Blood Brothers

Blood Brothers in Christ

MALCOLM SMITH

Fleming H. Revell Company
Old Tappan, New Jersey

Library of Congress Cataloging in Publication Data

Smith, Malcolm, date
  Blood brothers in Christ.

  1.   Covenants   (Theology)   I.   Title.
BT155.S6   231'.7   74–28018
ISBN 0–8007–0720–6

Contents

Foreword

The greatest outpourings of the Spirit of God in our generation are known as "charismatic." With praise and wonder we recognize that this means a specific experience: the Baptism of the Holy Spirit, usually with the accompanying sign of speaking in tongues. This is transforming individual lives, ministries, and whole churches throughout the entire spectrum of the Body of Christ.

How faithfully this same Spirit followed up the tempestuous outpourings of Pentecost with apostolic writings that gave foundation to the glories of the totally Christ-centered inner experience! Experience must be accompanied by understanding, and to the believers of the Early Church Paul wrote: "The eyes of your understanding being enlightened that ye may know . . ." (Ephesians 1:18).

I observe, therefore, with gratitude how God is doing just this among the charismatic brethren, in ever-widening circles. One of His present-day teaching apostles is Malcolm Smith. After his years of experience as pastor of the Salem Tabernacle of Brooklyn, New York (and his founding of a training school for the ministry), I am glad he can now answer requests to travel to the many churches and spiritual-life conferences for "the maturing of saints."

Malcolm Smith has put what he teaches into book form. His first was *Turn Your Back on the Problem.* Now he takes us the total way—first by thoroughly laying the foundation, then by raising the walls and putting on the roof. The result is a complete structure of what life truly is and how to live it. He puts the pentecostal experience into its whole setting. First he establishes it uncompromisingly in the abounding grace of God in His Blood Covenant. Then he reaches on and up into the glory of normal, daily living by opening up what Paul called "the special mystery now revealed to His saints" (*see* Colossians 1:26).This is where Malcolm Smith takes us —to what the psalmist called "the large place"—the hidden heart of the truth. This is sometimes missed, or presented in a distorted manner, by many preachers and Bible teachers. Malcolm Smith does not distort, nor does he leave us hanging halfway in a desperate effort to reach what appears to be unreachable. No, he takes us right to the mountaintop. And there *is* such a summit—where we squarely face the problems of personal living and find God's answer.

I need not say more; you will find it herein for yourselves. Bless you, Malcolm Smith, for finding the answer: first for yourself, through the Spirit and the Word; and then for transmitting it in simplified form to all of us, for those who have the knowledge can pass it on clearly to others.

NORMAN P. GRUBB

Introduction

The late autumn sun filtered through the leaves of the trees outside the window and made a moving checkered carpet on the mat on the floor where we sat and kneeled in an irregular circle. In the center of the mat was a large glass filled with wine and a small loaf of bread.

New York City was a long way off. The house was buried in the pine forest of the Adirondacks—far from the rush of the city. Three nights ago, we had driven through rutted forest tracks to this place, and had spent three glorious days in fasting, waiting upon God, and meditating in the Scripture. This was our last afternoon and we climaxed our stay with this service of Communion.

There was no stained glass of church building, no altar, no vestments, no pews, and no organ—but we had everything that was needed for the Communion. I looked around at the ingredients of the service. The fellows sat in their circle, most of them in dungarees. They had come from the streets, from Greenwich Village, and from across the nation. Raymond, an ex-junkie, now a saint in Jesus; Michael, artist, introvert who sat brooding bitterly in his room painting until he had been brought to the church, where he met Jesus Christ. Bob, a lay brother in religious orders who knew all the facts but did not know Jesus Himself. Brought to a prayer meeting in a home, he found himself surrounded by fellows and girls who really *knew* God, and were talking to Him, and were being delighted with Him. It wasn't very long before he had received Christ.

They, along with me, were the ingredients of a Communion service—sinners who had been confronted with what God had done for them in Jesus Christ, and had received it by faith—the living miracle that Jesus was alive.

On the floor were the bread and wine—the covenant meal that was the time-long reminder of that work which God had done for man through Jesus Christ. A broken body hanging on a cross, and poured blood, sealing forever a covenant between God and man.

It was no wonder that we had spent the last half hour, in fact most of the last three days, in worship. The song of praise that came from the lips and hearts of the group had died down and we sat with a tingling expectancy of God that came from the heavenly world.

I leaned forward and took the bread and broke it, saying as I did so the words of Jesus: "This is my body which is given for you . . ." (Luke 22:19). I passed the remains of the loaf to Bob, who broke off a piece and passed it on. Someone broke into the song that was taken from Isaiah 53: "He was wounded for our transgressions, bruised for our iniquities, the chastisement that would bring us peace was upon Him and by His scourging we are healed."

We were one with the cross of Jesus in spirit, and we knew again the love of God poured out in our hearts, assuring us in a way that surpassed all logic and reason that we were born of God, ones who had been died for and were now linked to God by faith.

We ate the bread in silence. There was a gift of the Spirit, a prophecy given by Tom, an associate pastor who was with us, and we rejoiced together oblivious of time. This was fellowship with the Father through the Son, and in the power of the Spirit.

I took the cup: "This cup is the New Covenant in My blood . . ." (*see* Luke 22:20). Drinking from the cup, I passed it on to Bob. In the stillness I quoted the terms of the New Covenant we were remembering from Jeremiah.

> "But this is the covenant which I will make with the house of Israel after those days," declares the Lord, "I will put My law within them, and on their heart I will write it; and I will be their God, and they shall be My people. And they shall not teach again, each man his neighbor and each man his brother, saying, 'Know the Lord,' for they shall all know Me, from the least of them to the greatest of them," declares the Lord, "for I will forgive their iniquity, and their sin I will remember no more."
>
> Jeremiah 31:33,34

A holy ecstasy went through the group like a wave. These people had been taught what the New Covenant was. They knew that this was a covenant meal we were partaking in, a meal that reminded them of who they were in Jesus Christ. They knew that they were the righteousness of God in

Him, that they had been delivered out of the authority of darkness, and that they were now in the Kingdom of the Son of God. We knew that the Age of Messiah had come and we reigned with Him as king priests. We knew the Holy Spirit as a person who sealed us in the covenant and was the taste of the glories to come. We knew that He was *our* God and we were *His* people. His covenant people, His chosen ones, now eating the memorial covenant meal and by faith reaching beyond the meal to the living Christ who was our covenant.

Our worship gradually subsided, but not before the sun had gone down behind the forest in a blaze of crimson golden glory, and the full moon had risen to make the pines stand out like black sentinels against the clear sky.

We stood outside and looked at the star-studded sky, a rare sight for a Brooklyn dweller. One of the boys raised his hands in the darkness and spoke, partly to himself, partly to us, and partly to God. "In covenant with the God who is the Creator and Upholder of all things, and in covenant with each other—and all that in Jesus. Wow! What a salvation!"

"You know," said Ray, "I went to San Francisco seeking life before I met Jesus. I had been a Buddhist in Nam, and I was all mixed up. I stood in the Colorado Mountains and saw God's work as Creator—and I remember raising my hands and saying, 'Who are You, wherever You are, I want to know You who made all this.' " He paused. "Now I know Him, hallelujah."

We walked slowly down the pine-banked trail to our cars, and drove back toward the great, sprawling, metropolitan area. The days of fellowship with God, the meal of covenant remembrance were not ends in themselves, dead ceremonies. It was going to work out on the streets of New York. Others were going to feel the power of God and speak words of life through Jesus Christ.

We cannot avoid the blood covenant. It faces us either directly or by implication in every story and miracle of the Scriptures. Any hope that we have of salvation can only be understood inside the framework of the covenant.

On what basis does a sinful man hope to approach God and find acceptance with Him? What audacity puts into our heads the idea that we may pray and receive an answer? Without a solid foundation faith becomes nothing more than pathetic presumption, a faith in faith which is a leap into meaninglessness. Biblical faith is a response to something God has done. God lays the foundation, takes the initiative, and faith is but man's response to that.

There is a solid foundation on which every promise and hope of salvation lies, against which every threat and warning becomes vividly real. That foundation is the blood covenant.

In its most simple definition a covenant is an agreement between two parties. But it is more than that, for it is the *union* of two parties in which all assets, talents, debts, and liabilities are held mutually. This agreement of unity is worked out in carefully defined pledges and promises that each makes to the other.

The Hebrew word for covenant, *Berith,* includes the idea of "cutting," hence the term *blood* covenant. Among all cultures, where the blood is shed in making covenant it is regarded as an unbreakable agreement.

The blood is the carrier of the life. We do not wholly understand it but, as the Scripture says, the life is in the blood (*see* Genesis 9:4), and to shed blood is to pour out life. In cutting covenant the bloods of the two are mingled, clearly saying that my life is poured out to you; we have now become one blood; our two lives are one.

The unbelievable news of the Gospel is that the Lord has entered into blood covenant with us and has pledged Himself to bless us within certain carefully defined promises. He has in fact given Himself away to us, calling us into union with Himself.

This immediately confronts us with a problem. Between equal parties a covenant agreement is fair and easy to understand. Two persons share their strengths and weaknesses, assets and liabilities, and produce in their union one strong person. But that could never be true of God and man.

How shall the Creator enter into an agreement with the creature? Even the breath with which the creature says yes to the covenant promises is given by God. How can the self-sufficient, self-existent One, the Eternal receive anything from man, the creature who derives all he is from the Almighty and in Him lives and moves and has his being? Man can only receive from God; he has nothing to give that is not already the Lord's possession.

The inequality goes further, for man is not only creature, he is the rebel of the universe. The highest order of being, self-conscious and with moral choice, he has chosen to make himself the center of the universe and pit himself against the Almighty. He has sinned against the being of God and thus opened the door for a thousand varieties of sins that are ultimately against the person of God.

Surely all this man can receive from God is justice, and he must be forever expelled from fellowship with God. With man the sinner how can there be talk of any kind of union? The One we would be united with is the One we have sinned against and He who is holy cannot walk with sin.

But the unbelievable Good News is that God *has* entered into a covenant with us. The Greek word for this covenant is *Diatheke,* which means, "an unequal covenant"—a covenant where one does all the giving and the other does all the taking.

In the person of Jesus Christ, God has taken upon Himself the penalty of the sin that we had sinned against Him, and in the shedding of His blood has wiped out our guilt, brought us into union with Himself, and given Himself away to us in certain carefully defined promises. He has brought us into an experiential union with Himself by placing the Holy Spirit within.

The Good News is that this *has been done.* He has taken the initiative and responsibility of saving us, and has done this in the work of Jesus Christ on the cross. All that is left for us to do is receive the covenant and at once the whole agreement of pledges and blessings is ours.

We can enjoy the *Berith* without understanding its whole message. Most of us walked into salvation without knowing all that we had walked into. But to know the truth is to be set free by it (*see* John 8:32). We are as rich and free as we know ourselves to be, and so as heirs of the covenant we must come to grips with its message of all that is already ours through God giving Himself away to us.

Generally speaking, the church has lost sight of the power of the covenant and hand in glove with that has gone a loss of boldness and authority in the receiving of the promises of Scripture. Wherever we have lost sight of our covenant rights there seeps in a sense of unworthiness and failure. We who were born again to be kings in God, speakers of the words of faith, too often live like beggars and die like paupers, not knowing that we are heirs to the greatest covenant agreement ever to be made on this planet.

In these days of revival we are learning a new confession. Instead of confessing our emptiness, inadequacy, and need we are learning to confess our fullness, riches, and supply that heirs of the Agreement have.

One of my students, after realizing who she was in the covenant, saw that although the same problems and needs would continue to face her, she now lived out of the endless supply of her covenant rights. In fact, all her problems were swallowed up in the supply. She stated it succinctly: "I do not have any more needs or problems, just opportunities to discover more of God's endless supply."

It is not enough to experience the Holy Spirit. In the Scripture He ever worked in conjunction with the Word of God. Our universe came into being on that principle. All was chaos and disorder. Then the Spirit of God moved on the face of the waters—but no creative action took place until the Word was spoken and then the Spirit united to the Word brought our universe out of nothing. Faith does not happen at the arrival of the Spirit alone. Faith is when the Spirit takes some Word from God and makes it alive to us. The foundation of faith is the Scriptures and therefore the Word of covenant.

The Holy Spirit took the initiative of grace moving on the chaos of our lives, and the Word of the Good News was spoken. We were born again by the activity of the Spirit and the Word. The Holy Spirit continues His work in our lives in proportion to the Word being spoken into us. For our faith to grow, and for the church to become the triumphant company that we are, we must have the Spirit upon us and the Word of covenant within us. So the twin epistles of Ephesians and Colossians state the two sides of the complementary truth: ". . . be filled with the Spirit" (Ephesians 5:18), and "Let the word of Christ richly dwell within you . . ." (Colossians 3:16).

Too many of us looked upon Sunday as the day when we reviewed our failures and anticipated our defeats. When we came to know the covenant, life became a week of delight interspersed with feasts of joy as we met with covenant brethren to confess in worship who we are. We know now why Paul could say that he was more than a conqueror through the One who loved him (*see* Romans 8:37).

Blood Brothers in Christ

1
The Sacred Berith

They stood opposite each other in awful solemnity, on either side of them a heap of quivering flesh. An animal had been split down the backbone. It was the solemn moment of *Berith*, or of cutting a covenant with blood.

It was always done over a dead victim, for it was an agreement that was loyalty to each other, even to the point of death. If broken it could be punishable by death. It was also a death to independent living, a coming alive to a new relationship in which there was a mutual holding of goods, person, and strengths as well as weaknesses and debts.

They were both young men, and had just concluded the passing through the pieces of the dead animal in a figure eight. One of the boys was deeply tanned, his features rugged from exposure to the sun and wind. His young muscles were like steel under his rough coat. The other youth was softer, with fine hands and a bearing that spoke of nobility. He slowly unbuttoned his richly embroidered outer coat and handed it over to the shepherd, following it with his belt and weapons. Prince Jonathan bar Saul was entering into a sacred *Berith* with David bar Jesse. The first step of that carefully defined ceremony was the exchange of coats and weapons.

A razor-sharp knife was taken and an incision made at the base of the right hand, which was then raised toward the sky. The blood trickled down, making a red river. The terms and promises of the *Berith* were made to each other.

They not only made their pledge to each other, but also to their unborn children. Jonathan was not yet a father, but all the children who were "in" him were at that moment represented by him. He was their covenant head. What happened to Jonathan happened to them. When David made the agreement, pledged himself in solemn promise to Jonathan, he did so knowing that Jonathan was the covenant head or representative of many children and that, at that moment, though they were as yet unborn, he was actually entering the covenant with them, too. Whenever they were born and came of age they could draw upon the person of David and all the promises made this day.

Having made the vows, they clasped hands and the bloods mingled as two lives died to independence and became one. The scar would be carried with pride by both of them. From that day on, if Jonathan was in trouble, David would react as if it were his own trouble. If David had a debt it automatically was Jonathan's debt, too. The scar would be the constant reminder of their unity and responsibility. Proudly Jonathan would call David his friend—the special title for a *Berith* partner.

They left the sacrifice and sat down to a simple meal, probably of bread and wine. It was the memorial meal of the covenant, demonstrating the transparent fellowship they had entered into, and now in fact enjoyed.

Years passed and children were born to the two *friends*.

They were tragic and dangerous years for both of them. David spent most of that time as a fugitive from Saul, Jonathan's father. Saul had a passionate hatred for David that had become a dark obsession urged on by demon power.

To begin with, he had tried to murder David in the privacy of the royal quarters. When that failed he organized a massive manhunt that drove David like a hunted deer into the caves and forests. During all of the time David never retaliated, but forgave Saul and preserved his life. The covenant between the two friends was tried to the limit, but throughout it was honored and secretly observed.

The entire family of Saul was drawn into the conflict. The obsession was like the vortex of a whirlpool drawing all into its suction. Their involvement to seek and kill David was only added to by a fear of what might happen if David retaliated.

David waited in the wilderness for God's purpose to develop, and Jonathan continued to raise his family at the palace. One of the children born to him was Mephibosheth.

Saul's attention was diverted by the Philistines, a pirate race who clung tenaciously to the coastland and made their brutal raids on the countryside, intimidating the simple farming communities. In a confrontation with them Saul and Jonathan were killed.

When the news reached the palace, mass panic broke out —a fear that was more of David than the Philistines. The family of Saul fled into hiding. One royal nurse was in the act of leaving the palace when she remembered her charge, Prince Mephibosheth, in his crib in the royal nursery. She took him and ran. In the blind panic she slipped, falling with the baby prince to the ground. Mephibosheth was to be a cripple, paralyzed in both legs for life.

A group of the family escaped to a desert chieftain, Amiel, who had a headquarters in Lodebar. In the dusty heat and scrubland of Judah, Mephibosheth was raised. In Hebron, David finally became king over all Israel and established his kingdom.

The young prince in exile was raised in the tradition of his grandfather Saul—antagonism to David. The wilderness headquarters was the center of plots and dreams looking toward the day when David could be dispensed with and a son of Saul placed on the throne.

One thing Mephibosheth did not know as he dragged his dead legs through the desert sands—he had been included in a covenant with the man he despised and hated—a *Berith* made before his birth but still in effect if he cared to reach out to take it.

David did not forget the sacred *Berith*. The covenant mark in his body ever took him back to when he and Jonathan (and all of Jonathan's unborn children) had walked between the pieces of the slain animal. He searched for the son of Jonathan, who could receive all the benefits of covenant. He found no clues as to where he might be. If anyone did know they kept sealed lips. They couldn't believe the son of Jesse had pure motives toward a son of Saul.

The information finally came from an old servant, Ziba, who told David where Mephibosheth was. It took no time for a company of the palace guard to be dispatched to bring Mephibosheth to David in Hebron.

At the sight of David's men and chariots, fear struck

Mephibosheth like forked lightning. He had never seen David but despised his faceless image with a passion, and also feared his power. Now the man who had haunted him since that hideous night of accident had summoned him. The David he had been told of all his life would predictably do one thing—kill him.

His dead legs dragged over the palace floor as Mephibosheth's crutches brought him before David. He was trembling now and prostrated himself before the monarch with the words, "My Lord David." He held his breath waiting for the death sentence. Instead he heard words that seemed to belong to a foolish dream where all the characters were mixed up. David was saying that he was about to restore to him all the lands of Jonathan and his grandfather Saul.

His mind raced. It couldn't be. The son of Jesse didn't have that kind of reputation in Lodebar. Words like that could be expected to be spoken to the loyal servants of David, who were now receiving as a reward the lands of Saul. It was something a person earned by faithfulness and long, meritorious years of service. But he was not a David loyalist. He was Mephibosheth bar Jonathan—who was supposed to be hated by David.

Thoughts churned incoherently inside of him. Everything he had believed was collapsing. What he had believed as truth now looked like a shabby lie. He was a prince in exile from David's government, an enemy who plotted against the throne, to whom the notice of David's death would have been the best news of a lifetime—yet he was now being offered all his possessions back and restoration to position. David continued, saying that he would treat him as his own son; in fact treat him as if he were Jonathan.

A sense of unworthiness swept over Mephibosheth that almost crushed him. He forced the words out of his mouth: "I am a dead dog"—a Hebrew way of saying he was worth less than nothing, no more than an embarrassing piece of garbage. What had he done to deserve this?

Nothing, Mephibosheth. This was not a gift based on merit. There was no searching through the files for a loyal soldier to reward. It was action based on faithfulness to a *Berith* cut before he was born, but which included him in it.

The mosaic pattern of the floor so close to Mephibosheth's face must have been an apt reflection of his thoughts. He was faced with the knowledge that his way of thinking had been proven totally wrong. Horribly wrong. The David he had believed in did not exist. Here was the true David, faithful to a *Berith,* full of pity and love. To admit that this was so would make him the barb of jokes and curses at Lodebar. The discovery of the existence of the blood covenant that included him added to the decision. It offered him his royal status, palace, riches, land, and it called him to become the *Berith* friend of David.

His decision was to become such a friend, dying to the life-style and way of thinking that had been his in Lodebar, and coming alive to a new life-style in union with David— to be friend to David as if he were Jonathan. He made that decision, although it could hardly be noticed in the realization that covenant had been cut.

When they helped him to his feet he was a different man. So new was the life ahead, it would take some time before he learned how to live in the covenant he had fallen heir to.

That is the true story of covenant, which can be traced in the Scripture story of 1 Samuel 18. Not all details are included, as the mode of covenant was understood by all. Not only does it define a covenant as it is understood in Scripture, but it also gives us a cameo picture of what the Bible is all about.

As surely as Saul was antagonistic to David, so the family of the human race is set against God. We have been raised in webs of lies that have been woven since the beginning of the race. All of us are afraid of God. The average member of the family of Adam believes that if ever God really got His hands on a man it would mean that we would lose something or someone we loved very dearly, and certainly the only way to really get to *know* Him would be to sacrifice all on a lonely mission in an African rain forest. This lie is so widely held as truth that it has even crept into the Christian religion's concept of God.

We didn't know that a *Berith* had been cut on this planet by one of the family of man, uniting us with God in sacred covenant. That one was Jesus bar Adam, but also Son of God, God in flesh. Such a person can be our representative. If one is to represent all of us, then he must be human in every way, actually a member of the human race, yet at the same time of infinite worth, who, because of that worth, could take into his person the race, making his history their history. Such a person was Jesus, Son of man, Son of God.

He was truly born of the Virgin Mary, actually of her humanity. He must have carried a resemblance to her in His face; He thirsted with our thirst, hungered with our hunger, slept with our weariness. He was no visitor from another

planet, a phony man, another being playing the game of
"Let's pretend to be human." This one is our brother, flesh
of our flesh, 100 percent human. He really faced temptation,
in which He made real choices and came out without sin. Yet
at the same time He is God, and as such can truly be the
representative man.

What happened to Him, happened to us. We were "in"
Him as Jonathan's children were "in" him. He is our cove-
nant head, our representative, and when He entered in a
Berith with the Father all that He transacted became ours.
All He accomplished *then* is our experience *now.*

It was as if the race stood in that one man. He carried us
into covenant with the Father in His person. All that the
Father is and has, is now given to us in our union with Jesus
Christ. We have become heirs of God and joint heirs with
Jesus Christ.

There is nothing for us to do, for all has been done in the
one representative, the covenant head. We behold what God
has done and we hear the message of covenant—that God
has given Himself away to us; He has Himself dealt with our
sin and now calls us into union. We make a response to that
message, trusting His word and receiving righteousness and
all spiritual blessings, not on the basis of who we are or what
we have done, but on the basis of who God is and what He
has done in the One who stands for all. All that we have is
because of our union with Jesus Christ, hence the constant
mention in the New Testament of the phrase "in Christ."

The night before the cutting of that *Berith* Jesus instituted
the covenant meal. The disciples asked no questions. They
understood the concept of covenant even if they could not

grasp the awful cost. This was the covenant of which all others were but shadows and suggestions.

In passing the cup Jesus stated that it was the meal of the *New Covenant* (*see* Luke 22:20). According to Jeremiah 31: 31, from which Jesus was quoting, the New Covenant is a *Berith* in which God takes it on Himself to legally remove our sins, write His laws on our heart by placing the Holy Spirit within our spirit, bring us to an immediate knowledge of Himself, and finally, to unite us with Himself. As He passed the cup to His disciples, He stated that in the shedding of His blood that would be accomplished.

It was accomplished when He went to the cross. More happened at the cross than the eyes of man saw. The physical sufferings were but shadows of the reality that was taking place.

Our sin is met in Him. He became sin for us, and the full punishment for all sin is swallowed up in Him. But more than the guilt of sin, *we* are there. Our problem is bigger than the sins we commit. The real problem is the self-centered sinner behind them. And so in order to accomplish covenant we are included in Him, and in His death the self-centered "I" dies, is buried, and in His Resurrection we are united to Him as our life, and receive of the Father the gift of the Spirit, who lives the new life from within us.

In that one person we all meet. God has dealt with our sins, carried the old rebellious us to death, and granted us the Holy Spirit—in a word, brought us into covenant with Himself—all in the history of the one covenant head, the Lord Jesus Christ.

The fact that it happened before we were born should not

cause us any trouble. God is not bound up in the envelope
of time as we are and in His ever-presence, what was then
to us is now to Him. Even from our human standpoint, a
Berith cut before Mephibosheth was born was still very
much in effect many years later.

In our experience today we all hide in our Lodebar from
God, and the Holy Spirit pursues us there, bringing us the
Good News of covenant. Lodebar is different to all of us.
Some of us hide from a real encounter with God in the empty
shell of an encounter. Our Lodebar is the rituals of a worship
that has long since lost the reality of God's presence. Others
flee from God into business, social success, feverish doing of
good deeds, and drugs and alcohol.

But the Holy Spirit finds us and we are made to see our
need and hear the Good News of what God has done for us
in Christ. It leaves us humbled and excited. The amazing
news of nothing to do, for all has been done! My only contribution is to say thank you and submit to the death of independent me—a death already died for me.

My response is to receive that which has been done and
take it as my own. It demands repentance, i.e. a radical
change of mind agreeing with God that I am the sinner and
deserve death. It is faith that sees that my covenant head has
not only taken that death but carried me to union with the
Father. I express that faith in baptism, the action of faith, the
outward seal of the covenant whereby I state the old me is
dead with Christ, buried, and risen to a new relationship with
God.

The covenant that God makes with us is always called a
Diatheke. The term *Berith* is always understood as such. My

thank you from a humbled, repentant heart is to the fact that I have been included in a *Diatheke* initiated, accomplished, and now effected by the triune God. This is the grace of God. It scraps all our frantic struggles to be right with God and stay right with God, and leaves us resting in God, who sets the terms of covenant and pledges Himself to achieve them.

2
Bobby

Bobby lay on the floor behind the sofa of the crowded apartment and listened, or tried to, through his reeling thoughts. He interjected a question here and there, willing his mouth to form the sounds he wanted to make. He was high on barbiturates and had been for months.

This was the first real contact he had had with Christianity for years—apart from going to church services at Easter and Christmas to please his mother. As a child he was forced to go to the church services every Sunday. Most of the time was spent in writing notes and chewing gum while waiting for the benediction.

When he was fourteen years old, a young evangelist preached to the teen-agers of the church. At the end of the sermon he pointed to Bobby and his friends, who sat unmoved and bored at the back, and told them they were going to hell unless they came now to the front of the church and repented. The boys were infuriated and embarrassed.

Crimson, Bobby rose to his feet and stepped into the aisle, not to walk forward to make a decision—but to walk out, making a decision never to set foot inside the church again.

The pranks of the gang led to smoking pot and experimenting with other drugs, until years later Bobby found himself hooked on barbiturates. He had a house to himself, as his mother spent most of the time caring for his aged grandmother. The house became the center for drug parties, and Bobby became a center for selling pills to support his own habit.

His body demanded more and more, and with the increase came the "gorillas," the result of too many pills over a period of months, causing him to become angry over the smallest detail, flying into a rage and fighting. This happened more than once and once it involved a fight with the police and an arrest.

And all the time his body cried out for more drugs.

There was an emptiness in Bobby that he himself could not define—a God-shaped vacuum that could only be filled by God Himself.

At this time he somehow came to a Bible study at the home of Peter and Ruth Noonan. I say somehow because he couldn't really explain how he or the others who were with him decided to go to the Bible study.

After the meeting he questioned the leader of the group, Floyd Nicholson, who was a minister. None of the questions made very much sense, but he was given sincere answers and he left—disturbed at the strange hunger that had been awakened in his heart. The rest of the weekend faded into oblivion at a party that left him stoned for three days.

The next week Bobby found himself back again and the next week, too.

The drug habit was claiming its victim. He was desperate for more drugs, and that week he went into his doctor's office trembling and twitching, threateningly demanding a supply of barbiturates. Seeing the boy's desperation, the fearful doctor gave him what he asked for. But Bobby knew he had come to the end of the road.

He could hardly remember what he had heard at the Bible study week after week, but one thing kept coming through —if he would give himself to Christ, he would be saved from what he was and saved to a new life, with Christ being his life. But he didn't really understand what that meant, either.

One thing stuck in his fuddled mind—although he still didn't understand it. He had spoken to me one night and had expressed that he would be a Christian, but he had a problem. He was an addict, he had four thousand dollars' worth of pills and grass in his house. My answer was to ask him what problem he would have with drugs if he were a dead man. He smiled and remembered saying, "I guess that would be the end of that problem."

I pursued my questions: "What would happen to all the stuff in your house if you were to die right now?"

Again he smiled and said, "I guess that would just look after itself." He remembered the shock when I said, "Bobby, if you will commit yourself to Jesus as Lord, that is exactly what would happen. Bobby, the addict, the pusher, the sinner would die with the death of Jesus, and a new Bobby would be—Bobby united with the life of Jesus, and that Bobby would need drugs no more, and the stuff in your house would just find its place." He smiled wanly, but the words stuck in his mind.

It was now Sunday, and Bobby called me on the telephone in my office. His voice was shrill as he said, "I want to get saved today."

I praised God and told him he could call upon Jesus right

there and be saved. "No! You are going to come to my house after the service tonight and you are going to pray for me, and I am going to be saved."

There was an arrogance in his voice that I did not like. It was Bobby snapping his fingers and calling the world to do his bidding. I was shocked to hear myself saying, "Bobby, I am not coming to your house. You can get saved right now, or you can walk a few blocks to the church. We have meetings all day." He slammed the phone down and I left him with the Holy Spirit.

After the service that night, I spent two hours with Karen, one of the girls who hung out with Bobby—leading her to an intelligent committal of her life to the Lord. I finally came out of the office at 11:00 P.M. and found a note stating that Bobby had called and wanted me to go and pray with him at 10:00 P.M.

As I got into my car, I wanted to go by his house, but felt an inner constraint that almost took my hands, turning the wheel of my car in the opposite direction. As I pondered it, I remembered the arrogance in his voice and I knew that there was no repentance. He was at the end of his rope, but he wanted to use God like a magic pill to counteract sin. The Spirit was telling me that at this moment Bobby belonged to Him, and he was being brought to true repentance.

I was awakened from a deep sleep at 1:00 A.M. to hear Bobby, hardly intelligible now, as he swore and cursed me. His last words stung me. "Okay, preacher, I am going to hell —and you are the reason. I wanted to pray but you were too busy. Well, I will never see you again—you can keep your religion." With an oath the phone was slammed down.

In the darkness I stood holding the receiver of the phone. Questions tormented me. Had I been right or had I made one of the most costly mistakes of my life? In naked faith I dropped to my knees and began to praise God, thanking Him that Bobby was in His hands, and He was now leading him to repentance. Such a peace possessed me that I knew there was nothing left to do—God was at work. I went back to bed and slept soundly.

After he had slammed down the telephone receiver across town, Bobby suddenly felt the helplessness of his situation. The pastor of his church and the leader of the Bible studies were his only hope. He had always felt that when things really got bad, they would pray with him and somehow everything would then be all right. He had enough Christians who were concerned enough to bail him out.

Now the receiver, silent on its cage, brought its awful message. He had said good-byes to the last concerned person. The last—because a few hours before he had physically put his mother out of the house and told her to leave him alone. His praying family, his praying friends—he had slammed the door on all of them.

He felt he was slipping into hell. He paced, he sat, and finally he crumpled to his knees and then on his face—alone before the God he had been fighting for years. His sin came up before him and he trembled as he whimpered, "God have mercy on me."

He suddenly knew what to do. Grabbing the telephone he called his sister. Because she was a member of the church, he knew she would be his lead. Out of sleep Joyce heard her brother crying for help—saying he was ready to die unless he had instruction and help in a hurry. Joyce called a couple of the men of the church who lived close to Bobby. Within minutes they were at his door. It was 3:00 A.M.

They told the desperate man the Good News: All had been done—Jesus was alive—and the moment he called on Him, Bobby would die and be united to the life of Jesus. His old life would be gone forever.

"How? My God, how? Sitting here with a fuddled mind, and every part of my body screaming. My soul in torment and despair—how?" The wild thoughts in his mind petered off as he slithered off his chair onto his knees. The men prayed, and Bobby prayed: "Jesus, save me now."

Suddenly he knew it was done. He was saved. He leaped from his knees shouting, "I'm saved!" The two men fell backwards, shocked by such a sudden, dramatic answer to prayer.

There was no doubt. Bobby was talking sensibly, clearly, and confessing that Jesus had saved him. He grabbed the phone and called his mother to tell her everything was all right—he had been born again.

I was awakened for a second time at 3:30 A.M. to hear Bobby shouting and laughing into the telephone—"Pastor, I am born again and I want to thank you for not coming around to pray with me. It had to happen this way." We made arrangements to meet the next morning and I went back to sleep praising God.

The next morning I met Bobby in a diner. His hands shook a little, but his eyes were shining with a brightness I had never seen before. He related the events of the previous night.

He smiled. "I had a call this morning from one of my

friends, and I tried to tell him what had happened."

"What did you say?" I asked.

"Oh, that was simple! I told him that Bobby died last night and not to call this number again!"

The wonder is that Bobby did not understand the covenant before he experienced it. He did not know *how* he could die until after he had died and risen again.

We need to know very little of the Good News to experience its power, but as soon as we have experienced it, we should learn at once what has happened to us—so that we can walk in what we have.

That morning in the diner I explained to Bobby the message of the covenant, that God had committed Himself with certain promises through Jesus Christ.

"He took it upon Himself to wipe out your sins, Bobby, and to give you the Holy Spirit to make you a brand-new person. In fact, the man you were is really dead." He nodded slowly as he finished his soda.

"It was there before you were born, Bobby, ever since Jesus shouted 'It is finished,' but like all of us, you didn't want to admit that you were so helpless and so sinful that only God could save you. You clung to some pride! You would still be the boss and let God save what you wanted to relinquish." His eyes brimmed with tears and I remembered his annoyance of last evening.

"Last night you were ready to admit sin and helplessly call on God and what He had done for you in the promises of covenant. Those promises were guaranteed to you through Jesus, and He kept His promise! As soon as you called on Jesus you were born again!"

The tears brimmed over and made little rivers down his face. "I had never seen it like that before," he said.

Within a few days he was baptized publicly, burying the old Bobby, who was dead. He went home, knelt beside his bed, and began to speak in tongues worshiping God.

For weeks afterward he went through withdrawals, and lay awake nights just praising God that regardless of his feelings, he was alive with the life of Jesus—which he was. The old life was rapidly disappearing and the new Bobby emerged. He is a member of the church today, married and praising God for the New Covenant that he enjoys.

We are not speaking of a beautiful theory, but of the final truth of the universe—the fact that makes all other facts into lies.

God has made covenant and whoever will claim it, repenting and confessing Jesus as Lord, will know its power.

3

Foundations

The idea of a covenant between God and man, in which man's debts are absolved and he is called into union with God, who has given Himself in promises to man, is not new to the words of Christ and the apostles.

We have one *Berith,* not two! It may appear upon a shallow reading of the Scripture that we have two subjects, on the one hand the nation of Israel with her sacrifices, and on the other hand Christ, His death, Resurrection, and Ascension, culminating in the church. But to see them as two subjects is to miss the whole point, for they are essentially one. Israel is the church of the Old Testament and the church is Israel come of age while the sacrifices of Leviticus find their fulfillment in the final sacrifice of Christ.

The one is the shadow and the other is the reality, but the shadow and the reality are essentially one. There is no contradiction between them. The shadow has an existence only because of the reality and is absorbed into the reality when it comes—so Christ and the ceremonies of the Old Testament. He is the reality that they spoke of and anticipated. When He came they found their end in Him, but they were the necessary sketch in earth of the heavenly reality which came to us in Christ.

The full bloom of the flower is Christ in His church. The vital roots are the dealings of God with the patriarchs and the nation of Israel. A root is sometimes very unlike the flower that grows out of it and it takes the Holy Spirit to show us that the root of the old covenant is finally expressed in the flower of the New Covenant.

Severed from the root, the flower is a cut, dead thing that fades. If we only see the New Covenant church without its greater context of the history of Israel, and the roots that reach back to the agreements made between God and man from the dawn of history, we shall only have a very beautiful, but rather awkward appendix to the history of Israel.

The fact of the *Diatheke,* God committing Himself to undeserving man in an unbreakable agreement, absorbing our debts at His cost, and calling us into union with Himself is not new to the Gospel. It is found from the beginning of man's history with God.

The covenant that most clearly shows helpless man resting in the initiative taken by God, and thus walking with Him, is seen in Abraham. The agreement between God and Abraham was not only the foundation of the history of the Old Testament but also the New. It awaited the New Covenant in Jesus Christ for its final realization. In coming to Abraham we come to the roots of the church and the beginning of our understanding of God's covenant dealings with men.

In the city of Ur in Chaldea the worship of the invisible God was almost nonexistent. On the whole the populace worshiped the moon, but being a center of trade, the caravans that came from the far north, from Egypt, and the ships that came in from the Persian Gulf brought their gods along with their wares.

One man should have been closer to the invisible God than any other. He was Abram, son of Terah. He traced his descendants through a line that worshiped Elohim back to Noah. But they were words and meaningless phrases that seemed very remote in a world of tangible gods that could be purchased at the bazaar.

It was a revelation to him of the glory of Elohim that woke him out of tradition to become aware of the reality of God. When God revealed His glory, He spoke to Abram clearly and directly. He was to leave his father and the family, leave his native city, and go to a land that he would be shown. He would become a great nation and through him all nations of the earth would be blessed.

The caravan moved slowly away from Ur; travel was not fast. It was in partial obedience to the voice that Abram went through the gates of the city, heading north along the fertile trade route that roughly followed the river Euphrates. It was obedience, for if he had been asked where he was going he wouldn't have known. He was following the voice and call of the invisible God. He expected further instructions down the path. It was partial, however, for behind his caravan was that of his father, and his nephew Lot had decided to come, too.

After a journey of many days they stopped in Haran, far north of Ur. They pitched tents and stayed, trading with the passing caravans. It was not the place God indicated, and no further communication came from God until the first was obeyed. It was only when his father died that the remembrance of the voice came urgently, and he packed tent and baggage, headed over the Euphrates, and came down into Canaan.

The silence from heaven had lasted many years—maybe as many as fifteen. But as Abram passed through Canaan, the voice came again, assuring him that this was the land that he had been directed to while still in far-off Ur. "This," said God, "is the land I am giving to your descendants" (*see* Genesis 13:15). Abram built an altar and worshiped God.

In the land he prospered and became a rich sheik. The years passed, and the promise from God did not materialize as the hair and beard grew grayer. To have descendants one must have a son, and it was too late for his wife to have children. The thoughts of the old man trailed away, always to end up staring at the words that God had said to him, now written indelibly in his mind, but unsupported by fact that eyes could see.

Would it be done *exactly* as God said? He sat in his tent and mused. Maybe he would pass on his inheritance, which consisted largely of the promises of God, to the chief and most trusted servant. That was a possibility that custom allowed to a childless man. Thus the old man sat among the camel cushions of his tent, his thoughts in a whirl.

One night as he sat the voice came again, quiet, clear, and compelling. It rose from within him, yet seemed to be all around him: "Fear not, Abram, I am a shield to you, and your reward shall be very great" (*see* Genesis 15:1).

The words were greater than he had ever dreamed before.

God was giving Himself away to Abram. He was saying that for anyone to touch Abram they would have to get through the shield, who was God, first.

In his worshiping wonder, the old man faltered. "That is all very well. You have made great promises—You state great things—*but I don't have any children* and how can any of Your promises be fulfilled if I don't have an offspring?" The question hung on the still air of the desert night.

Abram continued, "Do You mean that I am to pass my inheritance on to Eliezer, my chief servant? Is that how Your promises are going to come to pass? Is it his children who are going to bless the world? Tell me, Lord, is that what You meant?"

The Word of the Lord came directly. "This man shall not be your heir. One born from your own body—he shall be your heir." There was a moment of silence and the Lord continued, "Come outside." Abram felt a lifting from within and found himself moving out of the tent to stand in the cold desert night. He pulled his cape around him. "Do you see the stars, Abram? Can you count them? That is how many descendants you will have." Abram looked up at the velvet black sky studded with ten thousands of stars. In that moment he rested. He threw all on God (*see* Genesis 15:2–6).

His being here in this strange land, his saying that God would give him descendants—all of that was God's idea, not his. Then he would throw himself on God, and believe that He who said it could surely do it. He *would* have an offspring. In the offspring the world *would* be blessed. Great news, O world, for God would do something that was beyond Abram's natural thinking! Though his body was good as dead, his wife past the age of bearing children, they would have a child and through him the world would be blessed. He relaxed, accepted into the arms of God.

His communion had gone on most of the night. Now the Word came again, this time reminding him that He had brought him out of Ur to give him this land. In the gray light of dawn, he made out the shape of the hills, the dunes, the cacti growing silhouetted against the morning. It looked so impossible. This was land possessed by the Canaanites. How should Abram have a part in it? "How should I know, Lord?"

God spoke again: "Bring Me a three-year-old heifer" (*see* Genesis 15:9). As the command continued giving explicit direction, it dawned on Abram that God was calling for the sacrifice that went with the sacred *Berith*. The animals were to be cut down the middle and laid opposite. God was saying that He was entering into covenant with Abram and his offspring. Trembling, Abram obeyed. He had the Word of God and now was being given the Oath of God.

Soon the preparations were completed and the carcasses lay on the ground, the smell of blood hanging heavy on the sultry heat of the day. Black specks appeared and soon were swooping down, great birds of prey to eat the flesh. Abram spent his time most of the afternoon protecting the carcasses. No move from God brought his vigil to an end.

The sun dipped low and the sky turned indigo, and a drowsiness came over him. He sat down and was soon in a deep sleep. God's first move in cutting covenant was to put Abram to sleep, a very pointed way of saying that if Abram was to receive covenant blessing he made no contribution to it. He was at rest—very deep rest—the whole time! In a vision he watched the covenant being cut. A resting beholder!

He saw a Presence that he described afterward as a flaming torch. With a radiance like a white-hot oven, the Presence moved along the path between the pieces, the path that Abram would have taken if he had been participating in covenant. The radiant Presence was taking his place. The God of glory who had appeared to him in Ur was now walking through the pieces for him. God made the promise, and now God took Abram's place, making the promise depend wholly on God for its fulfillment; God promising by Himself that through the offspring of Abram all nations of the world would be blessed.

The covenant was based on who God was, not on who Abram was, or what he had done. Abram rested, believing God's Word and Oath and in so doing became heir to the promises that would eventually affect the whole world.

A short time after, in confirming the covenant Abram was given a seal in his body of circumcision. He and his descendants would carry the seal of the *Berith* in their bodies. At the same time Abram changed his name to Abraham, which means "the father of a multitude." He announced to the world that God's Word was as good as accomplished.

4

The Open Mouth

God had said to Abraham at the cutting of the *Berith* that there would be a time of great darkness and grief upon the covenant people before they came to the land promised to them.

Isaac, the miracle son of Abraham, received the covenant, as did his son Jacob. Jacob's name was changed by God to Israel. His twelve sons became the founders of the twelve tribes of Israel. One of his sons had become prime minister of Egypt and arranged for them to live in a section of Egypt called Goshen.

A nation in embryo, seventy people moved into that section of Egypt and settled there.

As the years passed, a change in government caused Egypt to adopt a new policy toward the shepherds of Goshen. Instead of enjoying royal favor, they were subjected to increasing slavery—finally under the cracking whip of the slave masters.

Even under the rigors of slavery they continued to multiply rapidly until, in fear of a rising from their slave population, the Pharaoh ordered that all male Hebrew children should be thrown into the river Nile. The river Nile was a deity of Egypt and the order was actually a demand that the Israelite children be sacrificed to the Egyptian gods.

The Israelites for the most part had forgotten that they were the people in covenant with the true God. They were greatly influenced and infected by the paganism of the Egyptians. They now turned to God and pleaded their covenant relationship. They realized that if they were in *Berith* relationship to Him then to touch them would be to touch God.

God heard their cry, not because they deserved it—they were deeply infected by idolatry—but because of the promise sealed in blood to Abraham, a promise that had been made on the basis of the coming Christ.

Egypt was the master of the ancient world. It was also a nation in the lap of Satan. The crown was worn by Pharaoh, and the symbol of his office was a snake, a fitting symbol for a nation held in the coils of Satan. The court advisors were magicians or witches, and demon gods ordered the lives of the populace.

Moses came as God's covenant deliverer. God's Israel could not be held captive by Satan! The situation was made crystal clear in the first interview when God gave His command: "Let My people go" (Exodus 5:1). The Israelites were uniquely *His* people and to touch them was to touch God.

Pharaoh greeted the command with laughter, and there followed a series of miracles, all based on the fact of the Israelites' covenant relationship, and each miracle snapped another fetter in the chain that bound them.

The first miracle happened as Pharaoh was on his way to the Nile. The river Nile was one of the demon gods of Egypt, worshiped as the giver of life. The Pharaoh was probably on his way to worship when he was confronted by Moses repeating the order to let God's covenant people go. This time the order was backed by turning the river Nile into blood. The God of covenant showed that He was God of the Nile and that it in itself was no god at all. In that one miracle the great god they worshiped was shattered. There followed miracle after miracle, each aimed at a deity of Egypt, until at last even the witches admitted that this was God at work.

The last god of Egypt to fall was the lord of death. The last miracle plague to strike Egypt was when the firstborn died and Egypt knew that this God was God alone.

Now Moses led the people—nearly three million of them —out of Egypt triumphantly delivered. One item remained to be filled of the Genesis 15 prophecy. It stated they would come out with many possessions. They had worked for generations without receiving a penny, and now as they left they asked their Egyptian neighbors for all their gold and silver. The Egyptians had a sudden wave of generosity come over them. They unloaded their gold and silver into the hands of the departing Israelites. The covenant people moved out toward the desert, rich and free.

But to a human observer the act of Moses was one of irresponsibility—leading millions of people into the desert with their flocks and herds with no water supply except what they could find in the wilderness, no food supply except what they could take with them, a blazing sun beating down, and the freezing desert nights—that was the height of foolishness. Added to that, the brigands of the desert, who were always looking for passing caravans, would have a simple task with the defenseless slaves untrained in warfare.

But it was not irresponsible, it was the act of a man who knew the authority of the *Berith*.

The covenant or agreement stated that they would be brought to the land and in that land an offspring would be born through whom the world would be blessed. It was God's initiative that had stated this, and God committed Himself to do it. They had not decided that it would be a good idea, but rather had been born with the contract of covenant already sealed that God would do this.

Faith never originates with man. Faith is a response to something. God has spoken His Word and bound Himself to keeping it by the oath of covenant. Faith is my response to that, saying, "Thank you, I have no idea how it shall be, but I choose to look through the problems and say it shall be so."

If the God who had committed Himself to them by the clear statements of covenant said they would get to the land of promise, then all the problems in between were not theirs but His who was their life in the midst of them.

Moses had learned the secret of letting God look at the problem through His eyes and accomplish what He purposed through them.

Their part of the *Diatheke,* this unequal covenant between God and man, was to receive what was given, not trusting their own ability—to be in fact helpless. They were receivers and speakers of God's words, walking out into the problems as if they were not there, understanding that the only truth was what God said, not the way things appeared.

The concept of covenant, two committed totally to each other, leads us to a strange formula: one plus one equals one. God + Israel = God living through Israel. Their needs were but the opportunities for God to manifest Himself.

Speaking of this period in history, Psalms 81:10 states that the call of God at that time was, ". . . open your mouth wide and I will fill it." A picture taken from the hedgerows—a nest of baby birds with their beaks wide open waiting for food. Baby birds are the epitome of weakness. All beak with a scrap of flesh on the end! In their utter weakness all they can do is open their mouths and receive what the mother bird supplies. The call of covenant was, "In weakness open your mouth and I will fill it." They were to take their place in the covenant and God would take His. They walked out into the desert with their mouths wide open to receive all that God would provide for them.

They needed a map, and shelter from the awful sun. As they came to the edge of the wilderness, God's presence among them was made visible in the form of what appeared to be a cloud by day, burning like fire at night. It hovered over them as well as at their head. Under that canopy they walked in their *Berith* Partner. In the shade of His glory no one died of sunstroke, and in His warmth, no one froze at night. As they followed the movement and the halting of the Presence, they were guided in safety. Their need of wisdom and protection was swallowed up in God's supply. In fact their need became a means of God manifesting Himself.

The first act of God was to lead them to a cul-de-sac. The cloud of Presence led them to the shores of the Red Sea until they were hemmed in by water on one side and mountains on the other.

It seemed a strange thing for their Deliverer to do! But there was more in God's purpose than a deliverance. He was teaching them to rest in their helplessness, drawing upon their invisible blood-covenant Partner.

They must be taught faith. They must learn in circumstances that baffle all human intelligence, wit, and muscle not to be afraid of the sensations of helplessness and fear. To be afraid of those sensations leads to panic. At such a time they must learn to respond to the situation by responding to God, who has committed Himself to be their all, and expectantly rest in Him.

While we are in easy circumstances that our intelligence and wit can handle we will never learn to helplessly rest in God and draw from His eternal resources.

Covenant people only learned the contents of the Agreement under pressure. It was the impossible that opened their eyes to see that God had already committed Himself to meet this need and that every emergency was the necessary cradle of a miracle.

And so their covenant Guide led them into a cul-de-sac.

Meanwhile Pharaoh had finished the protracted mourning for the dead that his religion demanded and it dawned on him that he had lost a nation of slaves. He pursued the Hebrews in haste with his own war chariots and six hundred besides as an immediate escort, supported by all the chariot force of lower Egypt with fighting men in each chariot. The trumpets echoed across the desert, accompanying the thunder of hooves and chariot wheels. An old Egyptian manuscript describes these horses as "swift as jackals, their eyes like fire, their fury like that of a hurricane when it bursts."

The Israelites were moving slowly toward the Red Sea. The waves on the shore could already be heard when the enormous dust clouds on the horizon told of the approaching army. Confusion broke out among the people. Terror vented in anger at Moses, mingled with a whimpering despair of ever getting out alive, spread rapidly among the tribes. Violently angry men hurled abuse at Moses, while sobbing women held their babies tightly and the distant thunder of thousands of chariot wheels gave the setting of mad panic and helplessness.

Open your mouth wide and I will fill it, Moses. Moses' voice was the only sound of sanity in the camp. "Do not fear! Stand by and see the salvation of the Lord which He will accomplish for you today—the Lord will fight for you while you keep silent."

The Lord's command to Moses was simple. He was to give the order to march forward *as if no sea were there* and to lift up his rod over the waters.

The cloud of Presence moved between the people and the Egyptians who were now bearing down on them. To touch the covenant people they had to first touch God. That awful Presence plunged them into confusion.

As the Israelites marched forward a terrible storm broke over the Red Sea, a wind blowing that opened the sea and made a path through. Walls of water towered on either side of the slowly advancing people as the sun went down over the desert. All night the evacuation went on.

In the morning light Pharaoh realized that again they had slipped his hand, and in blind fury ordered his chariots into the inviting path through the sea. In the middle of the water-lined chasm God caused wheels and axles to come off. Charioteers were shot from their chariots like stones from a sling.

In the midst of the confusion and moans the waters crashed down, burying the cream of the Egyptian army.

The next morning the Hebrews saw the piles of corpses tangled in chariot wheels and the paraphernalia of war all along the shores of the sea. Their captors were forever gone. The Israelites burst into a glorious dance and song to God for His deliverance. Around and around, they whirled in a sacred dance to God, exultant with praise, tambourines struck in unison, the women led by Miriam, sister of Moses, the men answering in praise to God.

But their walk with their God had only begun. They were to be further trained in dependence upon God.

As the vast caravan moved south the prospect was dismal. The skies above were glowing bronze with heat, the desert hard to the feet and strewn with sharp flints. Empty water holes had to be crossed; some trickled with salt-tasting water. Day after day and not a drinkable spring of water was to be found. As far as the eye could see, it was waterless and barren. It seemed to be the country of the dead. Nothing moved except the scuttle of a fleeing lizard, or a beetle disturbed from beneath a stone. Occasionally the bleached bones of a camel reminded them of the suicide road they were on. This was the wilderness of Shur.

They had waterskins with them but they were becoming exhausted. Thirst began to be their sleeping and waking nightmare. It seemed hard to believe that the radiant Presence was indeed their covenant Guide and Protector. It seemed that the cloud that glided ahead of them was leading them to bleach in this burning desert.

Suddenly water was seen and the people, half-crazed for

water, broke into a run, opening their mouths as they plunged into it. They came out spitting and gagging—it was salty and bitter—the waters of Marah. The rebellion that had smoldered in their hearts for days now exploded, and Moses again confronted the angry lynch mob that was ready now to return to Egypt.

Open your mouth wide and I will fill it, Moses.

Moses turned helplessly to God, calling on Him who is the supply hidden in every need if we have eyes to see. As he called to God his eyes lighted on a tree, which God commanded be thrown into the bitter waters. A miracle happened—the waters became deliciously drinkable. At this time God showed them that He would ever be their health as they obeyed Him.

When they had learned this lesson of trusting God for their supply in this matter of water, they were brought to an oasis where they rested, drank, and filled their waterskins.

It had been six long weeks in the burning desert since crossing the Red Sea. The supplies of flour and wheat from Egypt were running out; even the figs and dates from the last stop ran low. Famine now stared starkly at the mothers through the pleading eyes of hungry children. It seemed they never would learn that in all their problems it was really His problem; that every emergency was really the introduction to another magnificent miracle. They forgot every other miracle, disregarded the glorious Presence, and began to murmur against Moses.

Open your mouth wide and I will fill it, Moses.

With open hands Moses turned to Him who was about to manifest Himself their supply. The Lord gave the command that from then on they should go to the edge of the camp each day and there they would see the provision of the Lord. He would rain food from heaven.

The next morning an excited mob ran to the edge of the camp to be stopped short in their tracks. The ground was carpeted with a small, white, flaky substance. It looked like a frost had covered the desert. Someone picked it up and cautiously tasted it. Then another, and soon everyone held handfuls of the white stuff. They looked at each other nervously smiling. They asked each other in their native tongue, "Man hu?" or "What is it?" No one knew and so it was ever called manna, or "What is it?"

It was the daily provision of their God, supplying the need of His *Berith* family. Their need was but His opportunity of supply. (*See* Exodus 16:12–36.)

Their long trek was almost at an end. Ahead was the mountainous Sinai, with ample food and water for weeks and even months. But the local inhabitants were determined to resist their advance. They belonged to a Bedouin race known as Amalekites.

The last days for Israel had been grueling. The march had led through the granite rocks of the approach to Sinai. Granite heated by the sun became a burning reflector on the tribes as they passed by. To touch the rocks would be to scorch the hand. God had miraculously provided them with water, but as the Amalekites burst on them, the men were still weary and disorganized.

The swarms who came over the rocks were mountain fighters who knew every inch of the ravines and chasms. Desert warfare was their delight and the plunder of caravans their source of wealth.

Below them was a disorganized group of escaped slaves along with their women and children, who cringed fearfully. It was probably known that they carried with them all the gold and silver of Egypt.

The Israelites' greatest problem was their mass. They were on top of each other, and the women and children were in danger of being trampled before the Amalekites even got to them.

Moses quickly appointed Joshua, a young man of the tribe of Ephraim, in control of those few among them who could use weapons and they went out to meet the advancing mob.

Moses knew, and the people were coming to know that their part in this covenant relationship was that of weakness in order to express His strength. It was not for them to struggle or panic but to rest in God.

On this occasion Moses climbed to a rock that made him visible to all and stood with the rod of God raised.

It was a perfect symbol of what the covenant was all about —a man silhouetted against the sky, his hands raised to their God, who had pledged to bring them to the promised land. Not struggling, begging, or pleading, but looking expectantly to God to act. It was mute faith responding to God's Word with outstretched hands to receive.

The hours wore on, and Moses' arms were tired. He brought his hands down, and at once the army of Joshua began to be pushed back by the Amalekites. When he raised them again the battle turned in favor of the Israelites.

Realizing that their strength was their attitude of helplessness expressed in Moses, Aaron and his brother Hur came and held up his arms until the Amalekites fled defeated.

The event brought a revelation of their covenant God to them. He was known to them in their language as "Jehovah Nissi" or translated, "The Lord is my banner." As the enemies come to destroy us it is the Lord who fights our battles. We are in covenant, which means our problems are His problems, and He will fight for us. Whenever they were attacked in the future, any leader who called on this part of the contract found that that was the case.

5

The Law of the Covenant

The last three months they had covered approximately 170 miles of wilderness and desert scrubland. Every mile had given them fresh opportunities of abandonment to God as their covenant Partner. Now wearily the caravan of three million made their climbing approach to the Sinai mountain block, where they would make their home for the next eleven months.

A natural corridor led them to an enormous plain that was at the foot of the mountain. The plain was large enough for all to camp in. There was pasture for all their flocks; water springs and hidden glens were abundant in the surrounding valleys. Moses had kept sheep here for forty years until God had revealed Himself in these crags. They would have no worry concerning food or water for another year.

The northern end of the mountain rose directly out of the plain, a towering granite precipice. It seemed to form a natural altar. As they pitched their thousands of tents before this bare rock called Horeb, it was like the subjects of the great King assembling themselves before His awful throne that towered straight up into the sky. A few natural mounds at its base added to the scene, making the actual cliff untouchable by the people.

The southern end of the mountain was called Sinai, a gigantic granite monolith rising two thousand feet into the sky. Its central pinnacles, rugged and splintered, rose even higher. As the people stared in awe at the heights of granite piled up in chasms and torn rocks, a wild confusion of pinnacles, a natural awe gripped them, preparing them for this unbelievable year.

Valleys cut out of its stupendous form seemed to set aside the topmost crags, leaving them lofty and alone. Around these distant crags in the days to come they were going to behold their covenant God make known His will to man. They would hear Him speak as they gathered on the plain below.

They were now safely in the bosom of the mountain, shut in to hear their God and receive the Law from His voice and hand.

The cloud that had led them across the desert now settled on the mountain. The natural awe surrounding that place was overtaken by the Presence that now had everyone's attention. Unto the Presence Moses ascended, and returned to announce the words of God, the greatest news ever announced to a people.

It was a reaffirming of the covenant, this time with the whole nation. If they would keep His covenant they would be His unique and special people, His treasure on earth. He would be their God and King, and they would be His priests on earth. A call to covenant. With one voice the tribal representatives agreed that they would enter such a covenant.

The covenant would be cut as a sacred *Berith.* The solemnity of this one was marked by three days of preparation. The people were travel-stained and dirty. They must wash themselves and their clothes, and abstain from anything that would defile.

On the third morning the peaks of the mountain were veiled in thick, lowering clouds from which lightning flashed in a ceaseless display. It was as if the center of the shrouded mountain was on fire. The thunders crashed, rolling and reverberating from crag to crag. The multiplied echoes sounded like the gongs announcing that the covenant God was now here.

The mountain looked like a drunken man reeling on its foundations. It appeared to be smoking. Before such a sight the Israelites tremblingly withdrew to the farthest point from the mountain.

Moses went up into God's presence and spoke with Him in His manifest glory. In that God revealed Himself, in ten words, or ten commands. This was the God with whom they were in covenant. Moses heard His voice, and with His finger He inscribed the words on pieces of stone.

I am the Lord your God, who brought you out of the land of Egypt, out of the house of slavery.

Exodus 20:2

The words were Love speaking. Love had delivered them out of Egypt, guided them, protected them, had been to them their covenant Shepherd. He was not like the Egyptian gods so recently destroyed, who were mere symbols of nature. He was God of gods.

Unlike the gods of the Nile He was not a cold abstraction incapable of compassion. He who loved them was now speaking with them in a language they could understand, the communicating God drawing them to Himself in gentleness and love.

> *You shall have no other gods before Me. You shall not make*
> *for yourself an idol, or any likeness of what is in heaven above*
> *or on the earth beneath or in the water under the earth. You*
> *shall not worship them or serve them; for I, the Lord your*
> *God, am a jealous God, visiting the iniquity of the fathers on*
> *the children, on the third and fourth generations of those who*
> *hate Me, but showing lovingkindness to thousands, to those*
> *who love Me and keep My commandments. You shall not*
> *take the name of the Lord your God in vain, for the Lord will*
> *not leave him unpunished who takes His name in vain.*

> Exodus 20:3–7

He who is the original Person is invisible and therefore they must never make an image of Him. All their life in Egypt they had been surrounded by statues and representations of deity borrowed from the stars, animals, and fish.

He must now be revered and seen as the God so glorious that no image could ever be carved in stone. Even His name was to be treated with awe, being the expression of who He is.

> *Remember the sabbath day, to keep it holy. Six days you*
> *shall labor and do all your work, but the seventh day is a*
> *sabbath of the Lord your God; in it you shall not do any work,*

you or your son or your daughter, your male or your female
servant or your cattle or your sojourner who stays with you.
For in six days the Lord made the heavens and the earth, the
sea and all that is in them, and rested on the seventh day;
therefore the Lord blessed the sabbath day and made it holy.

Exodus 20:8–11

The seventh day had been kept from antiquity as a sacred
day. It was now given a new significance as a day set apart
to the Lord for spiritual invigoration as well as rest for man
and his animals.

It also carried a command often missed—not only rest on
the seventh day, but labor the other six. To walk with God
produced an industrious worker on earth, for he now worked
to God as well as rested to Him.

Honor your father and your mother, that your days may
be prolonged in the land which the Lord your God gives you.

Exodus 20:12

These were strange words in a barbaric society such as
surrounded Israel. In those nations, when parents became
old the children would often kill them, or leave them to the
wild beasts. Upon the death of the father the mother inevitably became subject to the eldest son.

Now parents were given a new status, and especially moth-
erhood was exalted as they would live their lives in God.
Their society would reflect their God at every level, beginning with family relationships.

You shall not murder.

Exodus 20:13

In the society of the ancient world, life was cheap, but man now was to see his God in the eyes of his brother and realize the sacredness of life.

You shall not commit adultery.

Exodus 20:14

The gods of Egypt and the surrounding nations encouraged sexual impurity as part of their worship. Many times sexual perversion was part of the religious ceremony.

God demanded a separation from this life-style. The word *adultery* is too narrow. The word in Hebrew includes all kinds of impurity as well as the specific of adultery.

You shall not steal.

Exodus 20:15

If man's life was regarded as sacred, all his possessions now took on a sacred character. To steal a man's property was to sin against God.

You shall not bear false witness against your neighbor.

Exodus 20:16

Absolute truth between man and man was demanded. It sprang out of the sacred dignity that these words gave to man.

All this was beautiful and right. No one could ever disagree. If there was a God at all He would declare Himself in these terms of love and holiness.

> *You shall not covet your neighbor's house; you shall not covet your neighbor's wife or his male servant or his female servant or his ox or his donkey or anything that belongs to your neighbor.*
>
> Exodus 20:17

The last of the words that came from God governed all the others. Without this the Law became an outward show with no real word to the heart of life.

"You shall not covet" addresses itself to motives and the coiled spring of who we really are behind all our actions and underneath our lip service. It confronts a man with the zoo of attitudes that lies just below the street level of our soul— caged beasts, some who will never see the light of day but who pace hungrily inside the imagination sending their cries through our desires. The hate and bitterness, the envy and pride, the impurity of mind, the fantasy of the imagination, a bedlam of lust demanding satisfaction.

A man may well have kept the Law outwardly and to the praise of his neighbor, but this command brushes past action and words to this other man who is beneath the surface and states, "You shall not even want to break the other commands," and in that instant all that man prided himself on collapses. He is discovered a sinner.

On that note the finger of God ceased etching on the stone. The Holy One had declared Himself, and in so doing had described to them the kind of walk and life-style His covenant friends walked in. The One who had spoken in majesty of love and awful, absolute righteousness called man into union with Himself, to be His people and to walk with Him in love.

A book of laws explaining the ten words was added. It breathed the same gentleness and care as the words just heard. In tender love it gave rights to slaves, to widows, and the poor; it called a man to care for his enemy in trouble and even gave directions that protected the rights of wild birds in the hedgerows. It was the Book of the Covenant. This is what life would be like if these people would walk in covenant with the Holy One.

It was a law of love that said, in fact, covenant people are to give themselves away to God and to their neighbor. Only then would man have true freedom, when chained by the law of love to God and man.

The Law was not to be looked on as a prison house in which man was locked up, but as a signpost on the road of freedom—much like a sign on the edge of a precipice road that said, YOU SHALL NOT JUMP OVER THE EDGE! Freedom and life are on this side of the sign!

Hidden in the command was promise. It was a call to *Berith.* God was calling these people to such a life and hidden in the command was God's promise that He would be their enablement to do so.

They had walked with this One in covenant since Abraham. Now He was introducing Himself and also describing the life-style of those who walked with Him. To accept the covenant was to say yes to such fellowship and such living.

Solemnly the covenant was cut. God was giving Himself away to this nation, and they were giving themselves to Him. They would be known as His people, the expressers in *their* weakness of *His* power; the containers, empty in themselves, to be filled with His fullness; to walk, a nation radiating the love of their covenant Partner.

To cut the covenant Moses, Aaron, his two sons Nadab and Abihu, and seventy of the elders of Israel were summoned to the mountain. They worshiped God. Moses went on into the Presence.

Down in the valley an altar of rough stones was built at the foot of the mountain and beside it were placed twelve stones as memorial pillars of covenant stating that each of the twelve tribes had accepted the covenant. Burnt offerings were made in which they gave themselves away to God, and peace offerings in which they praised and glorified Him were offered by a specially appointed priesthood.

Then came the actual cutting of the covenant. Blood was shed and half put in a basin, and the altar was sprinkled. The Book of the Covenant was read to the people.

They agreed to it. "All that Jehovah has commanded we will do and be obedient" (*see* Exodus 24:7). They agreed to walk in love, united with God.

The other half of the blood was sprinkled on the representatives of the people. They were sprinkled with the blood of the covenant that Jehovah made with them.

This ceremony answered to the cutting when the blood was exchanged in the *Berith*. They had become one blood. Blood brothers. Friends in indissoluble union. The blood poured in part on His altar and in part on the Israelites made them one with Him. They stood now in closest relationship to Him, abandoned to Him. He was their God and they were His people.

But was this an intrusion on what had gone before? A covenant had been cut—the way to God firmly established for nearly five hundred years. It was the way of faith and trust in God. It was the way of resting in God's initiative and action. Was this now a canceling of that way and the introduction of another way where a man worked hard at keeping the Law, entering and staying in covenant by merit and the sweat of his willpower?

That would be impossible. A covenant once established cannot be altered or set aside afterward. If two persons enter into a simple agreement, one cannot change the terms because he feels like it. So God, who is Justice, cannot by His own Being change the way of approach and fellowship.

What then is the Law? For although all men must agree on its beauty and holiness, agree that it is just and right, they have broken it in action, word, or spirit before they are old enough to read it.

The Law was given to show man how badly he needed the way of grace through faith. It lifted up to him in a concrete form the beautiful love and absolute holiness of the One he was called to walk with. It was not calling him to try and accomplish it by himself and show God that if he had tried hard enough he could imitate Him perfectly. It rather was to show him that this is what you must be—you will never accomplish it independently of God. Thus the Law drove man back to the covenant made with Abraham.

It drove man to despair regarding his guilt. Man knew that he was a sinner, but the Law showed it up—threw its white light on his life and showed him he was out of harmony with God, a god to himself, and a breaker of all God's freedoms in thought, word, or action, and thus lost and in confusion. It showed man his real need for God's unchanging love.

I look in the mirror every morning when I wake up. I know that I need a shave, but the mirror shows me the truth! I need a shave more than I ever thought I did. I do not then take the mirror off the wall and try to shave with it! The mirror drives me to despair of my condition—I cannot face the world like this—it also drives me to the remedy, the razor! So the Law is a mirror that drives us to despair. I cannot face God with my sin. It then drives me to the grace of God that declares God has already dealt with my sin.

The Law drives me to despair as to who I really am. We are blind to our true condition, and are privately convinced that we can be good, independent of God. We believe we can achieve it very well if we try hard enough, sure that wrapped up inside of us is all the goodness anyone could ever ask.

It is not surprising then that our first reaction to the Law is almost relief. It seems to be a marvelous alternative to the *Diatheke.* Now, instead of God telling me He has done all for me, here apparently is something much more sensible—I am called upon to obey commands and show Him just how good I really am.

At such a time the tenth command to "not even want to" is not even noticed as governing all the others. The commands are treated as a list of rules pertaining to my outward life so that so long as I do not actually kill my neighbor, I have kept the Law. But that is too easy, too many loopholes! So man makes it harder by adding many rules upon rules, but still misses the heart of it all—you musn't even want to.

This man gets a certain pride, a sense of being special because he has the rules and his pagan neighbor doesn't. At this point the man becomes insufferably proud, despising those who do not know the rules that make one acceptable to God. This poor fellow is certainly ordering his outward life by rules and disciplines, but inside he is unchanged. He finds that sin is rising up and wanting to act just the same. His actions are curtailed, but actually he feels more like sinning than ever.

He is to be likened to a dog who bites the legs of every passerby. The owners put a heavy chain on the dog and muzzle it. The dog doesn't bite anymore, but sits by its kennel coveting everybody's legs! The Law muzzles us and chains us, but actually we end up wanting to sin more than ever.

The Law has driven me to despair about myself. I am realizing the Law is for my inward attitudes and has shown me how to be a lawbreaker in the spirit of its commands. Is the Law an evil thing then? No, I say again, it is good, beautiful, holy, right—it has very effectively shown me that I am the wrong one. It has very effectively shown me that unless God saves me I am lost.

Here is a bull sitting lazily in the sun. He doesn't feel very much like a bull—he sits very docilely. Now someone begins to attract his attention with a red cape. Something begins to happen to the bull. He becomes disturbed, finally rising, and is soon snorting and pawing the ground. Was the red cape evil? No—it merely brought out the bullishness of the bull. It showed the bull what it was really like.

So the Law brings out all the sin that lies sleeping within us. The more it curbs our actions the more the Law stirs up sin within until in our helplessness to change things we are forced to turn to the *Diatheke*—God doing all in our salvation.

The Law brings one further note of despair. It cannot forgive. It knows of no forgiveness. Justice must be done. The sinner *cannot* go unpunished. It is always at odds with mercy, which says forget the punishment, pity him. The Law glares from its awful light, pointing its finger at us, demanding the just penalty of sin—eternal death.

We stand speechless before the Law. It is *right* that we cannot argue. If God damned us in hell He would be *right,* for we have broken the Law of the universe. We have risen up against the God of the universe.

This was the task of the Law. Such a man knows he cannot save himself; he is driven to accept the salvation that God offers, which is covenant in which God takes it upon Himself to pay man's debts and bring him to Himself. Even in the Old Testament this was the purpose of the Law—to drive people to see that their only hope was in the salvation God provided.

6

The Day of Atonement

The whole idea of a *Diatheke* is that One takes it upon Himself to fulfill all the terms of covenant. God has given man the Law, showing to him the extent of his debts. He also takes it upon Himself to wipe out those debts and write the Law upon the heart of man, bringing man into a perfect union with Himself.

The cost to God in bearing the penalty of our sin cannot be measured in earth terms. God shows us under the old covenant a little of that cost in the death of tens of thousands of animals in sacrifice.

But first man must be shown what he is called to—dwelling in the very heart of God, a fellowship with deity that is union with Him. On Mount Sinai Moses was shown the splendor and glory of heaven, and God gave him a pattern from which to build a tent on earth that would be a symbolic visual aid of heaven itself and the heavenly realm.

It was called the Tabernacle, or the tent of meeting. A simple structure, it had an outer court fenced by curtains. The entrance was a curtain at the eastern end, and upon entering, the first sight was a large altar of brass. Directly behind it and some feet away was a laver filled with water.

Behind the laver was the Tabernacle proper, a tent that housed two rooms. The first room was called the Holy Place and housed the golden altar of incense, which was in direct line with the brazen altar and the laver. To the right of the altar was a table with twelve loaves and a container of wine, to its right a candlestick with seven branches, the light continually burning.

Immediately behind all of this was the Veil, a curtain of tremendous thickness that separated the Holy Place from the Holy of Holies. This innermost sanctuary was lit by the Uncreated Light, the Radiant Presence of God who manifested His presence over a box that was placed directly behind the altar of incense. The box was made of acacia wood and was overlaid with gold. Inside was kept, among other things, the tables of the Law. The box had a lid of solid gold, beaten into two cherubim at either end who looked down at the top of the golden lid. This lid was called the mercy seat. This innermost sanctuary was barred to all. No Israelite could enter the Radiant Presence, not even a consecrated priest was allowed in, and the high priest could only enter on one most special day of the year. This Presence was God dwelling among His people, but even when He was closest He was inaccessible and distant because of sin.

That Presence over the box, symbolized by the box that contained the Law, was their covenant Partner who had revealed Himself at Sinai in the thunders. God is holy and man in his own merits and rights cannot enter His presence. It would mean destruction.

Every board, pin, curtain, and embroidered picture, as well as all its furniture, was symbolic of what Moses had seen when he entered that real heaven and communed with God. This Tabernacle was but a shadow of the invisible Real.

The Apostle John centuries later stepped into that same glory and described it in symbolic language. What he saw can be readily seen as the reality of what the Tabernacle was but a shadow. In Revelation 4 he described God in a flashing glory of transparent light with the burning red like sardius stone accompanied by thunder and lightning. He saw what the box in the Holy of Holies shadowed. As that box was in the center of Israel, so God is in the center of the universe in the white light of His holiness and justice, who by His very nature must judge sin. The Law given at Sinai is an expression of who He is. He is enthroned on praising spirits who worship Him: "Holy, holy, holy, Lord God Almighty . . ." (Revelation 4:8 KJV).

How can man approach such a God and live? How can man live in union with Him who is holy? God has taken it upon Himself in the *Diatheke* to Himself deal with our sin and assure the awful cost of our being made righteous that we might fellowship in union with Him.

He provided for their sin under the old covenant by giving them the priesthood. This was headed up in the high priest, who was given by God to be the representative man for all the covenant people. He carried the nation in himself, and in him they communed with God.

The essence of the priest's office was to bring man near to God representatively, through himself. So real was the connection between the priest and the believers that his being in the presence of God was for them to be in His presence. As the priest stood in the glorious Presence, he passed that on to the believers much the same as an electric wire passes a current. He drew the people after him so that in experience they were where he was.

In order to do this the priest had to be the same as the people in nature. He had to be one of them, taken from among his brother Israelites. He had to be exposed to the same problems and temptations and be able to actually carry his brothers in his person, feeling as they felt.

The priesthood officiated at the God-given offerings. For every spiritual need and mood of the people there was a provided offering wherein God took it upon Himself to bring the people to Himself. In all the offerings blood always had to be shed. Even the unbloody cereal offering had to be accompanied by one of the bloody offerings. The people must never forget that if sin was forgiven, it must be paid for with life given.

At the very center of the whole sacrificial system was one day that said everything God was doing in *Diatheke*. It was the great Day of Atonement.

The tenth day of the seventh month (approximately our October) was to be the day when the people brought their sins to remembrance. They were to look into the Law and realize the full extent of what they had done and who they were. It was a day of great sorrow that led to repentance. On God's side it was the Day of Atonement. He was providing the atonement, the covering for their sin, and bringing them into fellowship with Himself through the priesthood and the blood of animals.

All year long they had offered sacrifices for sin, but their imperfection still showed in that even after sin had been covered by the shedding of blood, still they were not allowed into the Holy of Holies, the house of their Father, God. But on this day the offering included all other offerings of the year and in a final sense summed them up so much that through this offering the high priest, as the representative of the covenant people, could go into the immediate Presence and commune with God behind the Veil. In his being there, every covenant Israelite saw himself there, carried in his representative.

The day began by the high priest taking off his beautiful robes and after washing, putting on the plain garments of white linen. His first act after this preparation was to take a bullock for himself and his family and kill it as an offering for his sin. With this blood he went into the Holy of Holies. He was a sinner, too, and before he could represent the people he must have his own sins covered.

He now acted as the representative of the people. Every covenant Israelite knew that in this one man God had provided the way whereby he could enter into the house of his covenant Father. If any of those Israelites who were seeing themselves in the Law were asked the way into the Presence, they would have pointed to the high priest and the blood of sacrifice. That was their way—in and through another.

Two goats were presented at the door of the Tabernacle. It was to be one offering in two parts. One was chosen by lot to be the sin offering, and was taken beside the altar for slaying.

If we were to ask the high priest what he was about to do, we would receive an answer something like this: "I am going into the Holy of Holies to stand in the presence of the Lord for you. In me you will hold fellowship with Him and enjoy all the blessings of the covenant for another year."

"Can I come, too?" I would quickly ask. Sternly the high priest would say, "No. I go alone, and then only with the blood of an animal shed for sin. You can never come except in me, your representative."

He then laid hands on the goat, symbolically transferring the sins of the people onto the animal. The people saw their sin now one with the goat. God had dealt with their sin in a substitute animal. A knife flashed and the animal was dead. The blood was caught in a basin. A sigh of relief might go up from the watching people, for at the shedding of blood the penalty of their sin was paid. The goat had died for them.

But that was only the first move. With the blood, the high priest went for the second time that day into the Holy of Holies, this time as the representative man.

He stood before the ark of the covenant and sprinkled the blood on the mercy seat. Just beneath that mercy seat was the Law that condemned all men as sinners. The blood was sprinkled on top—it was saying that the demands of the Law were met; sin had been paid for by death. Israel in the representative man could stand in Uncreated Light and worship.

The high priest was not allowed to sit down because sin was only covered. He knew he would be back next year in this continuing work where nothing was finished. He now came out of the sanctuary and returned to the people. His return told them that they were accepted in God's presence. But the ceremony was not yet over; there was the other goat still waiting at the door of the Tabernacle.

The *way* in which their sin was covered was shown in the

shedding of blood. The *result* of their sins being dealt with by God was now shown in the second half of the one symbolic ceremony.

The high priest laid his hands on the goat. It was actually a leaning, describing the burden of sin that was being laid on the animal. He then confessed all the sins of the people who listened, identifying with his words and seeing themselves polluting the animal. After a rope was tied about the animal's neck, it was led past the people to the wilderness. The people watched it go, knowing that it bore away their sin. They could *see* their sin going. What had been done behind the Veil in the shedding of the blood was now described in the goat that took their sins into the wilderness. When the man returned with an empty rope the people knew their sins had been carried by God into oblivion. They knew that God, against whom they had sinned, had taken it upon Himself to deal with that sin and bring them into fellowship with Himself through this representative man.

The last move of this great day was when the high priest put on his beautiful robes and for the people, again as their representative man, made a burnt offering. This particular offering was the one that described the mood of a man in normal covenant relationship. It said, "I am not my own; I am living exclusively to God and in God."

7

Taken to Father

This was the very best that any nation had in approach to God. It was what we now call the old covenant and was the way to God. In it God called man into union with Himself and dealt with his sin. But it was imperfect and insufficient. It was the root awaiting the flower, the shadow anticipating the reality who was to come.

That old agreement had all the ingredients, but fell short of the real and the true. Each part of its ceremony contained a hope, a promise of something better.

The representative man of Israel, the high priest, had to be a man taken from among his brothers. The high priest, however, was too much like us! He was a sinner, too, and therefore had to offer sacrifice for his own sins before doing so for the people. There was no guarantee that he would be a godly man or even be interested in spiritual things, for his appointment rested on his genealogy and not who he was as a man. It was also a very changeable situation because being a man he died, and the priesthood was constantly changed.

The offerings that he offered, though they were God's covenant act of covering the sins of His people, were insufficient and if they had any meaning at all, were promises of something better. How could an amoral, irrational goat take the place of man, a free moral agent who had chosen to rebel against God? Could such a man's sin ever be dealt with by an unwilling animal dying in a cause it knew nothing of? And all this took place in a tent that confessed to be only a pattern of the real heaven and was not itself the real thing.

As we have noted above, it was only a shadow of the reality. Shadow priests with shadow offerings moved in a shadow tent where people knew a shadow of union with the divine.

But wherever a shadow is, there is substance somewhere. The tent's very existence told them that somewhere there was a heavenly realm that was real and was at that time casting its shadows into our time-space world. The real is always spiritual and therefore invisible, and the shadows cast are material and therefore visible.

Somewhere was the real high priest and representative man of which all other high priests were but shadows. This One had a real offering that was the substance that gave all the shadow offerings meaning. Such a sacrifice would carry man into a real union with deity in the real heaven, which would be invisible, having dealt with sins forever.

That One was the offspring of Abraham, in whom God had promised in covenant with Abraham that all nations of the earth would be blessed. The blessing of that ancient covenant promise was the substance of which all this spoke.

Without this One who in Himself would bless the world, the shadows of the Israelite nation with its high priest and sacrifices would have no meaning. Shadows do not exist in themselves. The ceremonies of the old covenant had no meaning apart from the reality they shadowed. Because of the One who was to come, the blood of a goat could actually serve to cover sin until it be finally put away.

The One who was to come was the Radiant Presence that Abraham had seen take his place and pass between the pieces in covenant, for the fulfillment of the promises depended on Him. The Israelite people waited, looking for the offspring of Abraham to come, and in so doing they looked through the shadows and grasped the reality by faith.

The prophets even saw that age of glory when heaven would no longer be reflected into earth, but would come to earth; a day when the blessing promised to Abraham, the righteousness the Law demanded, the union the blood of covenant spoke of should actually be achieved.

Jeremiah saw a day of New Covenant which would be God achieving in man what the Law had demanded.

> "Behold, days are coming," declares the Lord, "when I will make a new covenant with the house of Israel and with the house of Judah, not like the covenant I made with their fathers in the day I took them by the hand to bring them out of the land of Egypt, My covenant which they broke, although I was a husband to them," declares the Lord. "But this is the covenant which I will make with the house of Israel after those days. . . . I will put My law within them, and on their heart I will write it; and I will be their God, and they shall be My people. And they shall not teach again, each man his neighbor and each man his brother, saying, 'Know the Lord,' for they shall all know Me, from

the least of them to the greatest of them," declares the Lord, "for I will forgive their iniquity, and their sin I will remember no more."

Jeremiah 31:31–34

Ezekiel saw an inward bath and cleansing and a life of the Holy Spirit within. If the real heaven came to earth it would be in the Spirit, for reality is Spirit, and man in that heaven would be in the Spirit.

Then I will sprinkle clean water on you, and you will be clean; I will cleanse you from all your filthiness and from all your idols. Moreover, I will give you a new heart and put a new spirit within you; and I will remove the heart of stone from your flesh and give you a heart of flesh. And I will put My Spirit within you and cause you to walk in My statutes, and you will be careful to observe My ordinances.

Ezekiel 36:25–27

Daniel spoke of a time when one would come who would cause all sacrifices and offerings to cease. This could only be so if sin had been completely dealt with.

And he shall confirm the covenant with many for one week: and in the midst of the week he shall cause the sacrifice and the oblation to cease. . . .

Daniel 9:27 KJV

And so the people waited for the offspring of Abraham, through whom all nations would be blessed. When the nation of Israel multiplied and became as dust and stars for the multitude, the people knew that there was more to the ancient promise than a nation. The Scripture says that they all died in faith waiting for the promise—the descendant of Abraham who should bless the world and in Himself bring about the New Covenant, the agreement between God and man that would forever deal with sin and bring man to union with God; the Radiant One who would pass through the pieces for man and give to him the blessings of the covenant. This representative man would take man in his own person into the presence of God, the true heavens.

One day the angel came to Mary in Nazareth and announced that this One would be born. He would be born of her and thus trace His descent to Abraham, but He would be born without a human father, for this was God entering the human race.

In the Lord Jesus Christ, God took it upon Himself to put away sin, to bring us into union with Himself, to make man an heir of God, and to cut the covenant with man.

Here then was the perfect high priest. He was perfect man and perfect God, the high priest, the representative man not based on genealogy but on personal worth. For the same reason He was the perfect sacrifice. Such a One who was God-man could take the place of all and bear the penalty of every sin.

In coming to earth He laid aside His garments of glory and in the simple linen of perfect humanity He came, the reality of which every shadow spoke. In Him every ceremony, feast, and promise found its fulfillment, to be needed no more.

Through His own blood, He the representative man would carry us in His own person through the true tabernacle, the invisible heavens, to be perfectly united with God in the Spirit: the everlasting covenant in which God has accomplished the bringing of man to Himself while man rests in His initiative and receives all through Jesus Christ.

On the eve of the cutting of the covenant and dealing with man's debts, actually bringing to the world the blessings promised to Abraham, He gathered His disciples together. He told them He was going away: the representative man, the high priest was standing at the door of the true, invisible tabernacle.

Peter asked Him if he could come, too. "Where I go you cannot follow Me now; but you shall follow later" (*see* John 13:36). He must go alone as the representativean, the high priest of the New Covenant.

The conversation continued, and Jesus revealed further where He was going and the purpose. "In My Father's house are many dwelling places . . . I go to prepare a place for you" (*see* John 14:2).

Before anyone can live in the immediate presence of God he must be prepared by having sin put away. This One was going to go to the real altar, and through sacrifice He would shed His own blood, cleanse away our sin, and thus prepare us a dwelling place in the Father's house, the Holy of Holies invisible in the heavens.

"And if I go and prepare a place for you, I will come again, and receive you to Myself; that where I am, there you may be also" (John 14:3). When this preparation had been accomplished, and in Himself He had prepared a place for them, He would come for them, uniting Himself with them that they, too, might live in union with Him in the Father's house, the Holy of Holies in the Spirit.

"I am the way, and the truth, and the life; no one comes to the Father, but through me" (John 14:6). Man of himself could never earn his way into the Presence, but in this representative man, all may come into experiential union with God.

He continued explaining to the incredulous disciples the results of this union. "Truly, truly, I say to you, he who believes in Me, the works that I do shall he do also; and greater works than these shall he do: because I go to the Father" (*see* John 14:12). Even as the Father had been expressed through Him on earth, so now He would be expressed through this company of covenant people through all time. God would be on earth in His all-love, His almightiness, and His creative Word. It would be them doing the works but the Source would be the God with whom they were united.

"And I will ask the Father"—He was their representative—". . . and He will give you another Helper that He may be with you forever; that is the Spirit of truth . . ." (*see* John 14:16, 17). The characteristic mark of that day would be the Holy Spirit imparted, who would unite them with God and take them into that realm of the heavens. This new day would be in the Holy Spirit.

He leaned toward them and they knew that He loved them: "I will not leave you as orphans; I will come to you. After a little while the world will behold Me no more: but you will behold Me; because I live you shall live also" (*see* John 14:18, 19).

The next hours they would feel forsaken and as if God had forsaken the planet, but actually in those hours the New Covenant was being cut, and when accomplished they would live with His life. It would be a day when they would know the union that He spoke of, when they would be caught up in fellowship with the Trinity.

"In that day you shall know that I am in My Father, and you in Me, and I in you . . . and My Father will love him, and We will come to him, and make Our abode with him" (John 14:20,23). Man exalted higher than his dreams could ever imagine—a fellow of the Trinity—the finite could not be exalted any further without encroaching on the infinite. A company on earth who live and move in a rest within the Father's house, in whom God lives, thinks His thoughts, performs His will, and is glorified on earth. This that could not be imagined at that moment would be known when He came again from preparing a place for them.

The little company rose from their table and moved on to the deserted streets of Jerusalem. They began to move through the narrow alleys to the gate that led to the brook Kedron, over the bridge and up into Gethsemane, from where they would watch as He went to prepare that place for them.

They passed the gates of the Temple, ornate with an enormous carving of a vine. "I am the true vine . . ." (John 15:1). He was saying that Israel was ever called God's vine, hence the carving in the proud monument only found its meaning in Him. He was God's Chosen One, the plant that would delight the Father's heart. He continued to outline life in the new age.

"Abide in Me and I in you. As the branch cannot bear fruit of itself, unless it abides in the vine, so neither can you, unless you abide in Me. I am the vine, you are the branches; he who abides in Me and I in him, he bears much fruit; for apart from Me you can do nothing" (John 15:4, 5).

There was no possibility of these or any men producing life that was pleasing to God—no possibility of man ever fulfilling his destiny unless linked by faith to Him, the representative man, who would then live His life through the believers.

He went from that conversation to the cross, and in the shedding of His blood put away our sin. Sin past, present, and future was laid on Him. As the ancient high priest burdened the goat with the people's guilt, so "the Lord hath laid on him the iniquity of us all" (*see* Isaiah 53:6). The shedding of His blood was enough. He put away sin and therefore the Father raised Him from the dead.

"Him who was delivered up [to the cross] because of our transgressions, and was raised because of our justification" (*see* Romans 4:25). Because our sin had been completely dealt with He rose again. Through that blood He would ascend into the real tabernacle, heaven itself, and carry us with Him there.

In the doing of that He visited with Mary Magdalene. She had come with the other women through the darkness of the very early morning that third day after He died. The skies were pink as they slipped outside the city to the tomb.

When they saw the stone rolled away, and heard the greeting of the angel who asked, "Why do you seek the living

among the dead? He is risen!" (*see* Luke 24:5,6), it didn't
dawn on them what had been said. Their grief made them
oblivious to the young man's words. They looked inside the
tomb.

They had been in there late before the Sabbath, winding
the linen strips around the lacerated body, putting perfume
and sticky gums between each layer. It had formed a solid
casing around the body. Mary remembered putting the separate strips around His battered head. The sight that met her
gaze stunned her. The case in which the body had been
wound was empty. The shell was there, but He was gone. The
headcloth was laid on one side.

A grave robbery! The women turned in panic to run back
to the city for the men. Mary lingered weeping at the ghastly
end to a hideous weekend. It was then that He came and
stood behind her, startling her. She spun around and, sup-
posing He was the gardener, begged Him to show her where
the body was.

One word from Jesus was enough. "Mary!" She recognized Him and clung to Him, mutely saying, "Never leave
us again."

"Don't cling to Me, Mary," He said gently. "I am not yet
ascended to My Father and your Father" (*see* John 20:16,17).

That sentence told everything. He had put away sin and
now united to Him, their representative man, they could call
God Father, even as Jesus did. They were included into the
Family through covenant. She must let Him go to the Father's house now, carrying them in Him.

He left Mary and went into the invisible universe which
is the Real and there was crowned King and Lord—and
declared a priest forever on the basis of who He was.

Therefore also God highly exalted Him, and bestowed on Him the name which is above every name, that at the name of Jesus every knee should bow, of those who are in heaven, and on earth, and under the earth, and that every tongue should confess that Jesus Christ is Lord, to the glory of God the Father.

Philippians 2:9–11

. . . when He raised Him from the dead, and seated Him at His right hand in the heavenly places, far above all rule and authority and power and dominion, and every name that is named, not only in this age, but also in the one to come. And He put all things in subjection under His feet, and gave Him as head over all things to the church, which is His body, the fulness of Him who fills all in all.

Ephesians 1:20–23

The reality had happened. Even as the high priest carried Israel into the Holy of Holies, so the Lord Jesus, our mediator of the New Covenant, carries us into the real Holy of Holies. Nothing more shall ever be done. He sat down at the right hand of the Majesty on high. Never again would a sacrifice or a priest be needed, for the substance was here.

But He returned from the Holy of Holies. He promised them that having prepared a place for them He would come again. And also there was the second goat.

8

Joined to the Lord

The atmosphere was a strange mixture of fear, skepticism, and excitement. The doors were locked, shutters drawn, for the little group of disciples were sure that they were next for execution. But then there were these reports of His Resurrection—the women from earlier in the day, and now the two had burst in telling how they walked to Emmaus with Him and sat to eat. The room was a buzz of conversation when one by one they stopped as they realized He was there. He had not come in through the door; in fact He had not made an entrance at all. He was just *there.*

They backed away, afraid, disquieted that they were seeing a disembodied spirit. Their mouths were dry in that awful silence.

He broke the silence. "What's the matter? Why are you doubting? Look, see My hands and My feet. It is I Myself: touch Me and see, for a spirit does not have flesh and bone as you see that I have" (*see* Luke 24:38, 39).

The atmosphere in the room was life itself. Who could describe the moment of creation? A new age was bursting into the world. An ancient prophet had seen this and cried, "This is the day which the Lord hath made; we will rejoice and be glad in it" (Psalms 118:24 KJV). These men who had lived in the shadows of the old covenant now saw the *real* high priest step out of the *real* tabernacle and confront them in a new order of life, time, and space. Fear and love of earth life fled before this fact of all facts. He lived.

"Have you anything here to eat?" (*see* Luke 24:41) The question He asked seemed oddly ridiculous. At such a moment when the chrysalis was broken and the glorious butterfly emerged—"Do you have anything to eat?"

One of the women, her voice cracked, dry, and high with emotion said, "We have some bread and fish." Woodenly she went to get it. He ate before their wondering eyes. He didn't need to eat, they needed to see Him. He was no ghost, but flesh and bone, glorified in Resurrection.

But there was unfinished business. He promised He would come back to them from the Father's house and certain things would happen when He did. They would be with Him where He was. Because He lived they would live also, a union with deity out of which His works would flow through them, His life expressed through them as sap through a branch.

That which had been accomplished by the shedding of His blood must now be made real and experiential to them. He came to each one, and breathed into them. In that moment their spirits came alive with the Spirit uniting with them. They were born from above. Where He was in the Spirit in the heavens, they were, too. The union was a reality; joined to the Lord they were one spirit with Him. They moved into the abiding place He had prepared for them in the Father's house. Though standing in a room in the physical universe, they now lived in the real Holy of Holies. The second goat!

What had been done was now experienced.

This is the New Covenant that the old had always anticipated—an actual experiential union with God. Living in God, God living in me. This is not just a good idea or a title. John wrote of this (*see* 1 John 3:1): "See how great a love the Father has bestowed upon us, that we should be called children of God; *and such we are.*" Through Jesus Christ we are actually made members of His family, alive with His life, or as Peter said in 2 Peter 1:4, "partakers of the divine nature."

The Gospel does not merely call us to believe certain facts that others do not. It announces to us that God has, through the representative man, done all He said He would. He has brought man into union with Himself, putting away his sin and writing His laws on his heart. Our new life is God in us.

Two Corinthians 5:17 states it thus: "Therefore if any man is in Christ, he is a new creature. . . ." Another translation is "new species." We may illustrate what we mean from a common tadpole. Each year the tadpole in our ponds undergoes a change. It grows legs, turns green, and becomes a frog. However, it is not a new species—rather a tadpole comes of age, for the frog was always wrapped up in the tadpole. The miracle of the New Covenant is not men come of age, a maturity that we grow into. It is rather a *new species,* like the tadpole becoming a canary.

Through what Jesus accomplished we are united to God through the Holy Spirit within our spirit. As we receive the news of covenant and confess Jesus Christ as Lord of all, and trust in Him who is the only way to the Father, the same miracle happens to us as to those disciples. Tadpoles turn into canaries. We become part of the new humanity. We become part of the new man.

God was taking it upon Himself to achieve inside of us what the Law demanded, not by helping us to keep the Law, but by placing the Spirit within us—uniting us to Himself, to His life. The New Covenant would be characterized by life within. The Holy Spirit inside us would achieve everything the Law ever asked for and more, but with no help from the Law.

A few months ago my wife went to England, leaving the two eldest children and myself to fend for ourselves. She had special concern for the children's survival—and so made sure that they were instructed from the moment the alarm went off in the morning.

A list of instructions was pasted to the mirror in the bedroom to make sure that they put the right clothes on, brushed their hair, and put their things away. Another set of instructions in the bathroom made certain they accomplished their toilet, and final instructions on the refrigerator door moved them successfully through breakfast, and then to school.

Now all that was very good. The instructions were excellent and could not be improved upon for harmonious living —but as all pieces of paper, they had severe limitations. Maybe the biggest was that homes were made to be more than places with lists posted all over the rooms.

Mother came home, and when she did we gratefully tore up all of the pieces of paper—with delight committing them to the garbage can. This did not mean that we were going to become a lawless household in chaos. It actually meant that something far better than instructions had happened— Mother herself! The instructions would be obeyed and all that the instructions aimed at would be achieved now—but in a way quite different from written instructions. The presence of Mother, who was the author of the instructions, made sure we did all of that—and more.

The Law was beautiful, but it had severe limitations and awaited the New Covenant when the Law on the outside, the list of instructions, would be laid aside—not that we would become lawless, but rather all that the Law had ever demanded would now be achieved—but without the Law—by the Author of the Law being within us. The New Covenant is union with life Himself, not trying to keep a list of rules and achieve life.

It is not the looking at the Ten Commandments and trying to keep them. It is not looking at the life of Jesus and trying to imitate it. All of that is me in the center of everything achieving a life, or seeking to. We have been brought into the New Covenant which is union with Christ, and His life through me by the Holy Spirit.

I was forcibly shown this in Africa when visiting a certain mission station. I was walking down a line of missionaries shaking hands with them, when I was suddenly confronted at the end of the line by a chimpanzee, grinning from ear to ear through clenched teeth, extending its hand to be shaken. It was an excellent imitation of a missionary—but all it produced was gales of laughter. The best that chimp could do was a very obvious animal imitation of a human. It was cute and entertaining.

When a human, out of himself as a source, sets out to imitate Jesus, he is just that—a human seeking to imitate a life that is life Himself, and the imitation would be laughable, except it is the essence of sin. It is man taking the place of Christ and saying, "Look, I can do the same—but all by myself without You."

The New Covenant takes the religious self-obsession to the cross and deals the death blow. The new, resurrected you in covenant has received the Holy Spirit into you to produce in you the life who is Christ—*not in imitation, but vital union.*

In the New Covenant, just as Jeremiah and Ezekiel said, that arrogant heart of stone has been removed in the death of Jesus. A new heart, soft and submitted to God, has been put within you—in fact the Spirit who is now within causes you to keep the laws spontaneously—or as Galatians 5:22, 23 puts it: "But the fruit of the Spirit is love, joy, peace, patience, kindness, goodness, faithfulness, gentleness, self-control; against such things there is no law."

Now this gives a different view of life. Life is not a series of things that I am aiming to achieve—rather life is the Person I am in union with.

Many people think that Christian living is like a mail-order catalog—I see in my New Testament the virtue that I am lacking and so I send away for it—I pray, plead, beg, fast, and cry to God for that certain thing I need—like love, or more joy, or power, or peace, or wisdom, or meekness. In my thinking I feel that God will suddenly give it and then I will be that kind of person.

The New Covenant does not state that. We do not receive a series of things—we receive Christ *Himself.* We get all things with Him, for He is all those things. They are merely earth words to describe certain aspects of Him. When the old me died, the Holy Spirit came to produce the life of Jesus in me. So I do not need to seek more things, but rather realize who is within me and let Him live out who He is through me.

He is life—and that cannot be imitated, nor can it ever become independently ours. It is not that we get a pocket of love one night as we are praying, but rather through the New Covenant we are *united to love Himself.* We do not get a special delivery on peace, but we are vitally united to Christ, who is our peace. That means that we can never have it apart from Him. It is not that we become in ourselves loving persons, but rather we learn to live in an ever deeper and complete union with Him who is love.

David saw this even in the shadows of the old covenant. The Psalms that he wrote are filled with such expressions as:

"The Lord is my light and my salvation" (Psalms 27:1).

"The Lord is the strength of my life" (Psalms 27:1 KJV).

"The Lord is my shield and my fortress" (*see* Psalms 144:2).

"Thou art my glory and the lifter of my head" (*see* Psalms 3:3).

He was expressing the union that he enjoyed in God. He did not say that the Lord is strong or is light. That would have been a true statement about God, but David was in union, which is far more than knowing something is true about God.

Nor was he praying to a distant God on the outside, praying that he would get strength or light or protection. He had no problem of getting God to him, for he saw that he was already united to God, and rested in that fact.

The Lord *is* my strength. He was saying, "The strength, the light, the salvation you see in me *is the Lord.* The union is so complete that my life is God in me. If that is so under the old covenant how much more in the New Covenant."

So many believers are faced with the problem of how to get God's life or eternal supply into us. Our constant search is for that pipeline that will bring God to us. We usually turn to the Law in the pursuit of this, seeking by fasting, praying, attending meetings of the church, and giving generously. Then God will, through that pipeline, come to us. That is nothing more than Law and will, as always, bring despair.

We *have* this union through what Christ *has* done. It is not something to search and look for. When we believed into Jesus we were united and we are now in actual union with God, married to Him in our spirits.

While we look outside for a means of getting Him into us, we are disregarding the fact that He is in us through the everlasting covenant. That union is not to be looked for but enjoyed. Facing the emergencies of life, we act as David did —*counting on the true facts.* "The Lord *is* the strength of my life."

Some Christians who have not yet really seen that all of this living is union with Christ, look at the whole affair as a storage battery. They store this thing called "love"—or "the victorious life" up very much as electricity is stored up in a storage battery. Frequent visits to the charismatic garage keep them "up."

No! The virtues are not to be stored—they are to be a

moment-by-moment expression of this Person. It is more like being plugged in to the flow of life from the socket. Unplug and all is dead. We never have anything in and of ourselves. We are the constant expressers of the Person who is our life.

This does not depend upon our feelings, but rather on what Christ has done for us. He has put that old me to death and He has become my life. Wherever I am, whatever I happen to be doing, He is my life. I do not have to be constantly reading my Bible, or in the physical act of praying, or having that other-worldly look on my face—just being me, He is spontaneously living through me.

When I face a challenge of life, or a call to sacrifice, or a call to the covenant way of life, I do not appeal to myself to try but to Him who is my life, that He will live Himself through me. Thus my life becomes an opportunity for Him to live. He is not calling us to a great act of will to struggle to be this kind of Christian and to keep ourselves living as He would—rather we let Him live.

This letting Him live becomes the essence of Christianity. *Life is not our responsibility, but rather our response to His ability.*

There is a picture that hangs in some homes of a girl clinging to a great rock. Most of her is submerged in the raging sea, and her hands are white as they cling to the rock. The caption is JESUS, ROCK OF AGES. This is a ghastly misrepresentation of the true Gospel. It gives the impression that I am struggling to keep up this union and to do all I can to stop myself from slipping. No! God has taken it upon Himself to bring you to death, and place the Spirit of Christ within you who lives His life through you—that is rest for you. A better picture to describe salvation would be of a person sunbathing on top of the rock—resting securely!

Through covenant, He is in union with you. Sometimes you feel that and thrill to it—and other times you are engaged with a million things of life—but you don't have to worry that He's no longer there because you stopped actively thinking about Him. It is not your thoughts about Him that hold you in union together, but the blood of the covenant shed at Calvary. You can rest in that and know that He is within, living His life at all times.

It was with this glorious end in view that the covenant moved through absolving our sins. Forgiveness is not an end in itself. It is God dealing with our sins in order to bring us to the heart of the whole matter, which is to *know* the Lord.

> And they shall not teach every one his fellow-citizen, and every one his brother, saying, "Know the Lord," For all shall know Me, From the least to the greatest of them. For I will be merciful to their iniquities, And I will remember their sins no more.
>
> Hebrews 8:11,12

The expression "to know" in the Scripture is used to describe the most intimate union on earth, the act of marriage. So we read, "Adam knew his wife Eve and she bore a son . . ." (*see* Genesis 4:1).

To know a person at any level is for life to have intercourse with life—the mingling of two persons. God is not a theory to be studied but the Person who calls us persons through the blood of covenant to know Him in the experience of intimate union.

When we believe the Good News of covenant in Jesus Christ we receive eternal life. That is not an endless extension of my living, but rather the taking of my life into union with God forever—a participation in God's life. Jesus said, "This is eternal life, that they may know Thee the only true God, and Jesus Christ whom Thou hast sent" (John 17:3).

Under the Law God spoke through men. Prophets spoke God's words, priests mediated God's message through the offerings and temple ritual, but the New Covenant states that no longer will man speak to man and say, "Know the Lord," for all will know Him from the least to the greatest (*see* Jeremiah 31:34). God will achieve for man an immediate knowledge of Himself.

9

Fred and Marie

It is to this most intimate union between ourselves and God that the covenant calls us. We are not called to merely know *about* God but to actually *know Him.*

Man is ever missing this, believing that by an intellectual accumulation of facts he can know God. This has produced the idea that because a man is raised within the walls of the institutional church, is duly catechized, serves some office within the church organization, and regularly attends the organized meetings of the church, he is thereby in possession of the knowledge of God.

He does not realize that though he may have a degree in theology, having an extensive knowledge about God, he misses this union with God, which is true knowledge, by a million miles. One may study Abe Lincoln until every detail of his life is known, but no one would equate that with knowing him.

When a man knows God he is not going through rituals aimed at finding, pleasing, or reaching a God who is "out there." He is not trying to arrive at the state of being right with God. Rather he is united with God and he knows it. He is living out of God's life, living out of love. Light is his source. Life Himself is his life. In this union he fellowships and delights in God.

It all began when Marie had a nervous breakdown.

Of all his virtues Fred prided himself at being in control, knowing where he was going. When his wife went into a tailspin of depression he didn't know quite where to turn. A young business executive with an office on Wall Street and a fine house and family in the suburbs, all had been moving upward toward success until Marie broke down.

It was decided that she go to an aunt and rest away from the noisy young family, but the twilight of the depression darkened to midnight. Days merged into nights without reason for being—until one morning of miracle.

It was early morning, with the dawn creeping out of the east. There was enough light coming through the window for her to see, and she reached out to take the Bible that lay beside her bed. She idly noticed that she had given it to her aunt many years before. Now she thumbed through it for no more reason than she did anything for a reason anymore. She stopped at John's Gospel and began to read. The words went meaninglessly through her head until she came to the words, "You must be born again" (*see* John 3:3). It was a message from God, a message of hope and answer.

"Of course that is what I need, a new life, a rebirth!" she exclaimed, excited for the first time in months. At that moment she grasped the words as her own, accepting the fact that the God who spoke the words of hope and command also was the Power to bring it to pass. In that moment she was born again.

She read the words again and again. As they poured over her darkened mind the confusion and emptiness retreated. Light dawned like the rising sun now streaming through the window. Tears of joy rolled down her cheeks in gratitude to God. A new life began as the depression slipped away like the dead leaves drop off at the advance of the new life of spring.

She returned home a new woman. Fred viewed her with relief. He was a little perplexed at her experience, but thoroughly applauded. "Just what she needed," was his comment to inquiring neighbors. In a sense he felt she was catching up to him. He had been raised in parochial school and college, served as an altar boy, and taught religious instruction to a group of unwilling boys. "Yes," he mused, "this is the best thing that could happen to her."

But as the days went by Fred saw in Marie a dimension of life he knew nothing about, a relationship with God that had no place in his code of doing your best to please God. He was mildly concerned at the anger that rose in him at the mention of Jesus Christ, in the way that Marie now spoke of Him.

A few weeks later Marie went to her room and prayed, "Our Father," and went right on praying in a language she had never learned. The Holy Spirit who had brought her to new birth now flooded her entire being.

She became possessed with a passion to know more about this Person she had come to know. The Holy Spirit made sure that she came to such an understanding. He drops questions and longings in our hearts just before He reveals the answers to us. If He didn't we wouldn't be ready for the answers when they came.

So He brought a couple across her path in an apartment complex nearby, Kaare and Helen. They had been in the Spirit-led way much longer, and Marie begged for Bible studies. She had picked up others in the spiritual pilgrimage and soon they met during the day to study, a group of housewives. But Helen knew there was more to be taught than she could lead into, and so she called me. We had been close friends since I came to Brooklyn, and his parents were members of the church.

I had never taken a home Bible study before and felt very nervous about facing so many different denominations. I could only think of doctrinal arguments and religious chaos breaking out. Wrestling with how to conduct the meeting, the Word came to my spirit: "Ask them if they know the living Jesus." Each word impressed itself within me. It only made me more nervous, for the idea of asking each one about their faith was hardly my idea of the first night of an ecumenical Bible study.

Fred received a pressing invitation to come, from Marie. He was aware of that anger again, almost as if he had been slighted. He felt very happy in his faith and didn't see any need to constantly rehash it. He had looked with mild satisfaction on Marie's daytime Bible studies. "She needs it," he told himself. "An alcoholic needs his AA meetings and Marie needs the Bible studies after that breakdown." But now evening classes that included men—from this he backed away. Added to that he was suspicious of me, as I was not ordained within his denomination and therefore suspect before heard. Fortunately he was able to say he was teaching church school that night and therefore could not come.

We got off to a late start, and Fred's school let out early. When I started Fred was sitting in the tightly packed living room. I spoke concerning the reality of the Resurrection and of the fact that we can know Him personally.

Fred was calm outside, but inwardly in a turmoil. This was beyond his depth. The church law, the details of the vestments he could argue about for hours, but this was water he couldn't swim in, and he felt the ground slipping from under him.

As I finished I asked the group, "Do you know that Jesus is alive?" No response was forthcoming; friendly eyes continued to look at me. Encouraged that no one was angry I turned to Marie and asked her the question. She responded with her testimony. Around the room we went, each one responding honestly and inquiringly. I came to Fred. "Do you know that Jesus is alive, Fred?" He smiled and started, "Of course, that's what—" He stopped with a strange look on his face, and then finished weakly, ". . . that's what I've always been taught." He stopped in a shocked silence. "That's it! *I have been taught* but I have never known it myself."

It was the moment of truth, the next step to life. In the following weeks Fred continued to attend the Thursday-evening meetings right on through the summer months. But he had dismissed the idea and plunged into his business involvements on Wall Street.

In the early fall Fred was sent by his company on business to Hawaii. He was a family man and did not enjoy being away, but looked forward to the balmy weather, the palm-lined beaches, and all that the company he came to do business with laid on for visiting executives.

At dinner that night he was told of all that was his during his stay on the island and he was rather shocked to hear that there was a girl included. He brushed the offer aside without any thought. He had never thought of being unfaithful to Marie. The suggestion was not even a temptation. The next night at the dinner, the girl escort was beside him. It seemed so natural to be driving her back to his hotel room a few hours later. He had rationalized all his objections away when a fear gripped him.

The Ten Commandments, learned in parochial school, and the accompanying sister giving a thrashing in the name of God loomed up before him. He realized he was afraid of God and what might happen. All his religious training and the concepts of right and wrong invaded him. He cringed in his seat.

As the car weaved through the cool night of the paradise island all hell broke loose inside him. A sweat broke out on his forehead and his hands stuck to the wheel of the car. A Fred he didn't know existed was making himself known.

He pulled the car to the side of the road and croaked out an apology to the girl through a dry mouth. Swinging the car around he dropped her off at her apartment and headed back to his hotel.

On his way to the hotel he choked up. Fred Casey, the altar boy, the church-school instructor in theology had sat in this very car beside a girl rationalizing that in his case it wouldn't be unfaithfulness.

In his hotel room he fell on his knees beside his bed and

sobbed. The Light that burst on Marie, who knew she was helpless and hopeless, had been healing Light. With Fred the approach of that Light was searing and devastating, bringing him to helplessness. He heard himself smugly saying, "Great, Marie, just what you needed."

He began to force his words out in prayer. "Oh God, if only I had taken that girl back because I *loved* You. But I took her back because I was afraid of You. I was just terrified of the consequences. *God, I don't love You, I don't know You.*" He choked on, ashamed and stung at having to have made the statement at all.

Another enormous step had been taken. He had seen that all he had was a list of rules that he was ready to break when it pleased him. That left no list of rules but rather Fred Casey —god. The horror propelled him forward.

When Fred arrived home he heard that I was in the hospital with cancer. Shattered that a young man his own age had such a lethal disease, he came to see me to try to offer some consolation. Instead we got on to talk of *him!* I asked him if he had ever read the New Testament. Rather sheepishly he admitted that he had only read parts of it and books about it. I gave him my copy and he went home promising to read it through.

Sitting down at the kitchen table he began to thumb through it. For no reason the binding broke. He was mildly angry. He hated books with a backing broken down the center. He looked at the page where it had broken, and his eyes lighted on "So then with the mind I myself serve the law of God; but with the flesh the law of sin" (Romans 7:25 KJV).

It was like an arrow that went through him and the night

in Hawaii came rushing back, with its awful discovery of himself that he had made, and here God confirmed it from Scripture.

He was angry. His pride was hurt and he found himself taking it out on Marie, who had returned from our church in Brooklyn. He found himself enraged, ready to throw her out of the house because of her faith.

To control himself he held on to the sink unit in the kitchen to stop the outburst. He began to shout, "Jesus Christ," again and again using the words in blasphemy. Suddenly he became aware that he was no longer blaspheming but actually crying out to that Name for help.

There was a way out, as the Scripture he had just read pointed out. It was through Jesus Christ. Through that One, God had taken it upon Himself to wipe out our sins, make us righteous, and bring us to union, knowing Him.

A broken Fred, knowing he was a sinner, turned himself over to Jesus Christ as Lord of his life. His sin was wiped out, the Spirit came within him causing rebirth, and he began a lifetime that would flower to eternity, in which he would come to know the One he now knw for the first time in his life.

But he had a problem with Marie speaking in tongues and talking of being filled with the Spirit. That was rocking the boat a little too much. One Sunday he knew that the matter had to be settled and went to visit with a local Spirit-filled priest, Father Jim Ferry. They visited and finally prayed together.

He slipped out of the church and went over to Kaare's apartment, where he and another brother were praying. Fred got on his knees beside them and as they prayed, all heaven broke loose and Fred was baptized in the Holy Spirit.

In that night of miracle Fred could never have explained what had happened to him except he knew he was not trying to be in God's presence, *he was there.* He was not appealing to any reason in himself why that should be, *he was resting in Jesus Christ.* He was not saying prayers to a distant deity in a perfunctory manner, but he was communing deep within his spirit to One he loved. As he walked through the evening mist he was walking in the new day that the Lord had made; he was rejoicing and being glad in it. Though he was the newest member in the covenant family, God was keeping His Word: ". . . all men shall know Me from the least to the greatest" (*see* Jeremiah 31:34).

10
Covenant Memorial

The fact that we are now in covenant means that God has now placed Himself at our disposal, has made us new creatures, His dwelling places. The promises of God are not for display but to be actually taken and used.

It is not a matter of pleading or begging for God in mercy to give. The covenant means God *has given* and now we *are* heirs of God. It is but to receive and praise. He has committed Himself to us and we now belong to Him to be the expression of this union on earth.

A young girl ran through the heather. A light mist hung like a veil above the moor, and she shivered in the predawn air. Drawing her tartan shawl around her she quickened her step.

She was on her way to a Communion service to be held in the crags above the moor. Hundreds were secretly making their way there, risking their lives in so doing. In Scotland at that time it was a crime punishable by death to believe in the free grace of God. The British redcoats were ready to capture and execute any who worshiped God in a way other than king and Parliament ordered.

A group of Scots who had seen their relation to God in covenant had covenanted among themselves to be faithful. The covenanters were again risking their lives this morning to meet together and break bread and drink wine in the covenant meal.

The girl scrambled over the rocks and suddenly was surrounded by British redcoats, who had been alerted that the covenanters were meeting somewhere that morning. "Where are you going at this hour of the morning?"

She was in a dilemma. Tell a lie she couldn't, but to tell the truth would mean death and torture for hundreds up in the crags. She decided to stake all on the theological ignorance of the soldiers. "Sir," she said, "my elder brother has died. I am going to hear the reading of the will, and claim my share of the inheritance!"

The soldier patted her on the head and let her go on her way, blissfully ignorant that she had just described a New Covenant meal!

We may call it Eucharist, or the Lord's Table, or Communion, but we are describing the memorial of the New Covenant, the meal that comes at the end of any *Berith*. At the *Berith* memorial meal, all the terms of the covenant are seen as my own, and the fellowship arising out of the covenant is enjoyed.

The Jews had met each year and eaten the Passover, the meal of the old covenant. Jesus had taken the unleavened bread and the cup of wine and made it the meal of the New Covenant.

So we gather to eat bread and drink wine. We do so in remembrance of Him, proclaiming His death (*see* I Corinthians 11:25,26). It is a time of unspeakable joy. Remember Him, and thus remember our representative man. We cannot remember Him without remembering us, for we are one together. In so doing we proclaim, declare, preach His death —in the cutting of the covenant we are declaring who He is, what He has done, and who we are in Him.

Every time we commemorate we are saying, "I am in covenant with the Father through His blood. I live unto God in His life. My sins and my iniquities are remembered no more. I have a new heart, His Spirit is in me, my life. I know God, and I know that I know Him. He is my God and I am His person and one with His people. I have this through His grace. I am accepted because of Him." This we proclaim every time we eat and drink.

To put the bread and wine to our lips is to state that we are blood-covenant heirs and all the riches of covenant are ours. It is the act of faith when before devils, angels, and men we state who we belong to, and who we are in union with. We reach beyond the bread and wine to the realities in the invisible and it becomes to us the step of faith from the visible appearances to the invisible realities.

The blood-covenant man assailed by doubts and accusations comes to the table of Communion and his faith reaches to the blood. He whispers, "Thank You, Father—all my sins are wiped out through the blood of Jesus. I am made the righteousness of God. I take now what is mine." The Spirit witnesses to his confession, and he rests in the peace of God.

Such a meal is the moment of high praises to God. The prophets saw what we would be privileged to live in and expressed it in the most joyous terms:

To grant those who mourn in Zion, Giving them a garland instead of ashes, The oil of gladness instead of mourning, The mantle of praise instead of a spirit fainting. So they will be called oaks of righteousness, The planting of the Lord, that He may be glorified.

Isaiah 61:3

And the ransomed of the Lord will return, And come with joyful shouting to Zion, With everlasting joy upon their heads. They will find gladness and joy, And sorrow and sighing will flee away.

Isaiah 35:10

Or, as David expressed it, "Thou hast turned for me my mourning into dancing" (Psalms 30:11). We now look directly at what He has done for us and realize that we are those who, through the *Diatheke,* live in Zion, and we worship in unspeakable joy and glory.

It took time for me to see that. I was taken as a boy to an assembly of very sincere Christians who looked sadly at one another like spaniel dogs. They had come to remember His death and they conducted their regular funeral service—that was what I always thought of as a Communion service until I read that we remember *Him* and join the new man in joy-filled praise in stating our union.

The man struggling with temptation and longing to grow in Christ puts the cup of wine to his lips and praises God for Christ, his life. He is no longer the old man he was, but he is the new man in Christ. He worships the Father, who is being glorified in him.

The blood-covenant man who is sick takes the bread and praises God that by the scourge of Jesus he is healed. At his confession that reaches out to the health that is his in Christ, the same Spirit that raised Jesus from the dead makes alive his mortal body. In our services of Communion where we have numbers of people who understand and reach beyond to the realities that are theirs, we often have a person healed in the taking of bread and wine.

It is in this that we rejoice in the fact that we know Him. It is the love service of memorial, when the family worships. It is the priestly family ministering unto the Lord.

The blood-covenant community meet and in their utter dependence reach out to Him who has stated that He is their God. They go from there to the world to be the expression of God's glory in their neighborhood.

To take the covenant memorial with an enlightened understanding is to know what is written in His will and covenant to you, *and to take that for yourself.* It is the moment of confession as an individual and as a community. We join with the churches on earth and in heaven around the Lamb:

And they sang a new song, saying, "Worthy art Thou to take the book, and to break its seals; for Thou wast slain, and didst purchase for God with Thy blood men from every tribe and tongue and people and nation. And Thou hast made them to be a kingdom and priests to our God; and they will reign upon the earth."

Revelation 5:9, 10

We become aware that we are in harmony with all creation and orders of being who are praising God with us, and we sing with them:

> And I looked, and I heard the voice of many angels around the throne and the living creatures and the elders; and the number of them was myriads and myriads, and thousands of thousands; saying with a loud voice, "Worthy is the Lamb that was slain to receive power and riches and wisdom and might and honor and glory and blessing." And every created thing which is in heaven and on the earth and under the earth and on the sea and all things in them, I heard saying, "To Him who sits on the throne, and to the Lamb, be blessing and honor and glory and dominion forever and ever." And the four living creatures kept saying, "Amen." And the elders fell down and worshiped.
>
> Revelation 5:11–14

We step out into the sunlight of this planet to be who we are in Him.

11
Don't Say No to Temptation

To understand the covenant, to walk in the light of the fact that God has made an agreement in which He commits Himself to be our life and has spelled this out in His unbreakable promises through Jesus Christ, is to adopt an entirely new life-style: a life-style of drawing from the All-Sufficient instead of looking at life as a pauper begging at the rich man's door.

We are now ready to understand how all temptation is for us. As covenant children, united to God through Jesus, we cannot be battered by trials or crumble under the circumstances. We see them now as part of our riches to be taken and used for our development.

A man who has seen the Agreement can intelligently praise God *for* trials and temptations as well as *in* them. He has seen that all things work in harmony for the development of the heirs of the covenant.

These words, trials, temptations, and tribulations have various meanings to each one when we say them, but in the original language it is summed up in the one word *test*. This is to be understood very much as putting metal in a testing chamber to see how strong it is.

You see, I have believed into Christ. I have believed into His death and He is now my life. It is to this that my faith is anchored. Now although that is the new me, my faith must dominate my entire life. My mind is so used to thinking in terms of the old-self way that it is a conflict at times between my spirit, which is the residency within me of the Holy Spirit, and the flesh, the combination of soul and body, which will always have the tendency to go off and do its own thing.

There must be the process of renewing my mind so that it is not set on the flesh, which would swing again to independency. My mind must now be trained to come under the dominating faith that has laid hold on the cross and Resurrection as its own.

God's way of training is to expose area after area as weak and helpless, and force it back on the finished work of Jesus, and His being our life. Our dependence on ourselves is constantly discovered and brought under the death I have died, and begins to operate in life.

The gentle way He does this! He does not make us giants overnight—He gradually brings all of our weak points into the light and forces them to death and resurrection. Of course, weak so far as He is concerned; many times we think they are strong points. There are areas of our independency where we feel we can handle the matter. In such areas our trust in ourself is strong; our faith in Christ our life is very weak.

Now we must go through a process whereby we discover that weakness, so that we view it as God does, and also a process that drives us to choose to die to our self-sufficiency on that point and become strong in the faith that sees that self dead—and sees Christ our life at *this* point. That process is that of temptation, trial, tribulation—or the better word, *testing.* One Peter 1 calls it the testing of your faith.

A set of circumstances or an arrangement of people are sent into your life, and their presence brings out certain weaknesses and shows the condition of your faith at that point.

The devil is allowed to tempt you so that your faith may be discovered for what it is, and also that it may be strengthened by positive rest in Christ at this point.

The Word is used and illustrates what we mean: Jesus had been speaking for three straight days and the vast multitudes were hungry, nearly fainting. Jesus turned to Philip and said, "What shall we do to feed this multitude?" He threw the problem into Philip's lap. Now, said John, who wrote the account, you must understand that Jesus knew what He was going to do, but He did this to *test* Philip. He deliberately walked Philip into a set of circumstances in order to really see where Philip was in his faith. There was a lot of talk and enthusiasm, but Jesus wanted to see where Philip really stood in relation to his faith in One as his all.

Philip grabbed his pencil and pad and began to count and work out. He finally said, "We've got a problem! Two hundred pennyworth of bread wouldn't be enough to feed this mob."

Philip! He failed the test. He should have known by then that he couldn't run off from himself as a source to solve the problem—rather he should have put it back in His lap and the problem would have become a magnificent unveiling of God. Well, of course, that's what happened anyway, but in it Philip had learned a very self-sufficient spot where his faith was weak.

Now Jesus wasn't surprised or shocked. He knew that anyhow. Now Philip knew what Jesus had known.

It was the same with Peter. Jesus said to him that Satan desired to sift him as wheat. I would expect Jesus to reassure him that He had forbidden Satan to touch him. Instead, He simply said, "But I have prayed for you" (see Luke 22:31, 32). In effect: "I have given permission and through the test, I have prayed for you."

As Peter sat in Pilate's judgment hall and blasphemed, he discovered what he was capable of when left to his own self-sufficiency. He was shocked and stunned. He thought he was stronger than this. Oh, no, Peter! He had only found out what the Lord knew all the time. He had miserably failed the test, but he was not thrown out of college. He now, with his great weakness discovered, would start developing his faith and living out of Christ his life and not out of himself.

How shall we who live the blood-covenant way live then? We must learn to handle temptation so that we are working with it to achieve God's purpose.

When temptation or a set of pressing circumstances arises, I have a certain response within—the Bible calls it lust. This is a word that suggests evil desire today—but actually only means strong desire. Let us understand that the strong desire is not sin. It is what a man does with that strong desire that determines whether or not he will sin.

If I walk past a steak house, I have a certain glandular reaction—my mouth waters. That does not mean that I have sinned. However, if I obeyed that strong desire every time, then I would be guilty of the sin of gluttony. But there was never anything wrong with the desire.

However, it is at this point that many are crushed. They ask, "How come I get such terrible thoughts?" or "How come I am tempted as I am? If I really was dead with Christ, I wouldn't have these desires." At this point Satan's strategy is to mock with such words as these: "There, if you were really a Christian, as holy as the New Covenant says you can be, you would never have such wicked desires."

But of course, Satan is a liar, and that is a total lie. The old man is dead, but you, your personality, your natural desires and reactions are still there and may rise in response to stimuli. It is learning what to do with these desires that will cause them to become beautiful containers of Jesus, or to fail miserably.

Well, what do we do? I have pointed out that it is the trying of our *faith,* not our *willpower.* Our first reaction to temptation is to start reacting just as if there were no blood covenant.

I suddenly start operating back under the Law. I appeal to a command that forbids the temptation and I appeal to my willpower, which says, "Now I will not do that, I mustn't, I will please God."

Now even if I succeeded in avoiding the temptation I would have failed the test. All I would have done is to reveal that I have a strong willpower. This is the testing of our faith, it is leading us to the free flow of the life of Jesus.

We must learn not to merely say no to temptation; it must be in the power of an enormous *yes* to Jesus, who is our life.

Every test must be looked upon as another beautiful opportunity to die in experience to my own self-sufficiency and to let Jesus be my life. So when temptation calls the strong desire to rise within, I do not go struggling against it, exercising my willpower alone, but I recognize the truth: the old me who would have responded to this is really dead with Christ. This temptation is allowed in order to establish me in Christ, my life. Lord Jesus, live Your life through me at this point.

You will be surprised at the peace and victory that you immediately enjoy. It is the peace and victory of Jesus, your life. You *are* united to Him and that becomes an actual experience when you call upon it, acting as if it is true.

Now let your attitude toward life be in the light of that. You are not the person you were—you can now live the life of Jesus, not by trying, but by letting Jesus live it by putting on His life. Chapter 4:1 of Paul's letter to the Ephesians begins this thought, and it is taken up in full in verse 17 of the same chapter. He states what they *were but no longer are.* That kind of person in verses 17–19 is the one who died with Christ.

Very well, Paul, what do we do when we are faced by the rising of some of these very things within us? Do we assume then that we are not really dead? Never! We know the *truth* is that we have certainly died—that these feelings are not the true us, for the true us is living out of Christ our life. So we put them away, refuse them in the light of who we really are in Christ, and then put on Jesus Christ—draw upon His life, recognizing that the new life is not a struggle, but a flow— not me trying to achieve, but rather a union with Jesus. It is not a matter of merely saying no to temptation, which would be a battle of willpower. It is rather saying a great YES to the Christ who is my life.

Watch how Paul puts it in Ephesians:

> Put off your old nature which belongs to your former man-
> ner of life and is corrupt through deceitful lusts, and be
> renewed in the spirit of your minds, and put on the new
> nature, created after the likeness of God in true righteous-
> ness and holiness.
>
> Therefore, putting away falsehood, let every one speak
> the truth with his neighbor, for we are members one of
> another. Be angry but do not sin; do not let the sun go down
> on your anger, and give no opportunity to the devil. Let the
> thief no longer steal, but rather let him labor, doing honest
> work with his hands, so that he may be able to give to those
> in need. Let no evil talk come out of your mouths, but only
> such as is good for edifying, as fits the occasion, that it may
> impart grace to those who hear. And do not grieve the Holy
> Spirit of God, in whom you were sealed for the day of
> redemption. Let all bitterness and wrath and anger and
> clamor and slander be put away from you, with all malice,
> and be kind to one another, tenderhearted, forgiving one
> another, as God in Christ forgave you.
>
> Ephesians 4:22–32 RSV

Notice that he is assuming on the basis of what he has
previously said—that now you *can* put off that old way
because it really is no longer you. You can put on a new way
because you have put on the life of Christ and He lives
spontaneously through you.

In the fall, the old leaves drop off because the tree is dead. Any leaves that do remain on the tree we all know are no longer part of the tree—it is dead. When the new life begins to push through, the old leaves that cling are pushed off.

Nowhere is the Bible calling us to a list of negatives. It is rather that the new life, who is Christ, is spontaneously expressing Himself, and the old is being thrown off.

It is not merely that we have stopped this or that—rather having thrown off the old we are now learning and expressing the new.

Thus says Ephesians:

> And do not get drunk with wine, for that is debauchery; but be filled with the Spirit, addressing one another in psalms and hymns and spiritual songs, singing and making melody to the Lord with all your heart, always and for everything giving thanks in the name of our Lord Jesus Christ to God the Father.
>
> Ephesians 5:18–20 RSV

It is not simply that I don't drink anymore—but having put off drunkenness, I am now in dynamic union with Christ and being filled with the Spirit.

The blood-covenant man grows in the intimate knowledge of Christ and goes on from strength to strength, manifesting the glory of God through union with Christ his life.

12
José

The Agreement that God has made with us through Jesus Christ is complete, perfect, and now ours. We can walk through life in our union with the Father and for every sense of weakness and inability know that Christ is our life and strength. Covenant people have no needs, just opportunities to let Christ live through them.

We can be very bold in this because in covenant the Father has *committed* Himself to us and waits to keep His word to us.

It is no wonder the early Christians called it Good News, for it is the greatest news man has ever heard. In fact, in the minds of many it is too good! They feel there must be a struggle somewhere; it would be presumption to believe that God has *done* all and *is* the all. The agreement that God has made with us is to rest forever in God as His possession. Our only activity is to work out what He has done.

For most of us it takes time to see how this all works out. It is in the laboratory of temptation that we slowly learn that it is not a matter of struggling and thrashing, but rather a drawing upon the strength of God our covenant Partner.

Such a case was José.

We stood in the filthy room that reeked of urine and garbage. I bit my tongue to stop myself from throwing up. In the hole that had once been a window was a soggy, lice-ridden, half-burned mattress to keep out the elements. The whole room was black with smoke from a fire that half-gutted the place some time before.

On the floor were hundreds of little white bags that had been full of heroin. In the corner was a bottle of water, and strewn in that corner, burned-out matches. It was a "shooting gallery" where heroin addicts came to shoot heroin. A few moments before, I had followed José along dimly lit hallways where two people could hardly pass. After leaving the sunlit streets outside it seemed darker than it really was. In these ratholes overfilled garbage cans stood outside of doors that let into even murkier holes, where people lived out some kind of existence. Where there were no garbage cans, there was just garbage. These passages reeked of rotten garbage, wine, and the smell of death.

As we climbed upward, we came to a corner where a bright lamp hung starkly from the ceiling, revealing the dark green paint on the walls, with names and messages carved into the plaster.

José turned, and I saw his olive face smiling. "Scared?"

"I wouldn't choose my vacation here, that's for sure!" He laughed a deep chuckle. "Next floor, I'm about certain."

The next floor had some empty rooms and I saw what lay behind those doors—just a room that would serve as a closet in some American homes, with a smaller room to the side. I shuddered as a rat fled from under our hurrying feet.

José was standing before a door that had lost its handle

and had its surface gutted by frenzied boots kicking to open it. He cautioned me to stop and be still. He knocked softly. There was no answer, so he kicked his boot where many others had been.

The door burst open, and the stench of garbage, urine, and vomit came out and engulfed us like a wave. I felt a nausea and swallowed hard.

José breathed heavily as we stood surveying the evil place. "This is it—but no one is here." We had come hoping to find some friends of José, but the place was empty. The burner was still warm, suggesting that heroin had recently been cooked.

A faraway look was in his eyes. He motioned to the corner. "I used to sit there every day—sometimes three times a day —and shoot the stuff."

"Dear God," I thought, "no wonder he got hepatitis. How could any needle be clean in this place?"

We stood there and began to quietly worship God for the blood of everlasting covenant. José had been an addict in Spanish Harlem, where he now stood, and had been dying from hepatitis. He came face-to-face with the Gospel. It was too good to be true—that Someone loved that bag of skin and bones. Someone had died for him who deserved to die—and Someone had risen to become his life.

José knelt in the Teen Challenge chapel in Brooklyn and received Christ as his Lord and José *died.* He didn't know anything about the covenant in so many words, but as he received Jesus Christ he believed into the covenant without knowing all about it, came to the death of the old him, and a new José stood to his feet alive with the life of Jesus. A little later he was filled with the Spirit and we met him in our church.

It wasn't long before he realized that although he was a new José, he still had strong temptations to return to the old ways. He was tormented, as we all are.

"If I am really dead, how come this happens? If I am saying no to all desires for heroin, but still it keeps coming —have I got to endure this for the rest of my life?"

One day as we talked in my office, I asked him, "What do you do, José, when you get those desires to go back to the needle?" He looked at me a little surprised, almost hurt. "What do you think I do? I say no, of course!"

"That's your trouble! Never merely say no to temptation! Say YES to Jesus!"

He looked mystified. "What do you mean?"

"Look José, when Jesus died *you were in Him*—that was you, that old junkie and sinner José. You were there in Jesus. Right?" He nodded. "When you believed upon Jesus, the Holy Spirit made that *real* and *vital.* You came alive with the life of Jesus. No more you running your life. A new Lord was life." He nodded slowly, taking it in step by step.

"When you were baptized, we were burying forever that old you and stating to the world that you have believed into your covenant Head. So now your Christian life is Jesus living His life through you, not José trying to be like Jesus, or trying to please God, or trying to imitate Jesus—but Jesus Himself living through you.

"So when you are tempted it is not an opportunity to try hard to say no—but rather an opportunity to recognize the real truth—this is not the new me, I have left this way, I have put it off, Christ is my life. Live your life through me now!

So it isn't your willpower saying no to temptation, but saying YES to Jesus, who is your life."

He nodded with eyes gleaming. "I see that," he said.

He brought me back to the filth in Harlem. "You know, pastor, I feel like a visitor from another planet. I can't believe that I used to come here—that this was my life."

"You're right, José, you *are*. You are a dead-alive man. You who came here really died—you exited, then you rose again—only the risen one was Christ-in-José. You came back here a person who is in the world, but not of it."

My mind turned back over the months to a time of great trouble for José. Just learning to walk in the covenant and still not having fully grasped the principle I had shared with him, with the pressures building up, all he could think of was a fix of heroin. He said no—and put the thought out of his mind. But it came back, and came back. "One fix and you'll forget your troubles," was calling inside like a broken record.

He worked on Times Square, and traveled to work by subway each day. One morning, someone asked him a favor —would he deposit eighty dollars in a bank on Broadway for him? He walked to the subway with the eighty dollars burning a hole in his pocket, and the euphoria of a fix burning a hole in his imagination. He slumped in the seat of the train, shaking his head, wishing he could shake his thoughts out in so doing.

As the train screeched into the Fifty-ninth Street station, he looked up wearily to read a poster. Opposite him was an advertisement from the mayor's office. It pictured a bag of heroin and a needle. The words blurred as the picture fastened on his imagination. He knew he could never walk across Forty-second Street station with eighty dollars in his pocket, and pushers a few feet away, and a craving that gripped his mind. He had forgotten that urine-vomit-filled room where heroin had dumped him. The strange call seemed to come from deep within, fanning through all his senses. "Dear God, help me," he kept whimpering from a more real self within.

The train came to a grinding halt at Forty-second Street and Times Square station. José sat rooted. He became aware of a sweat trickling down his face on a winter's day—cold sweat of fear. "I daren't get up and go out there. I can't say no anymore."

The doors of the train opened like the pit of hell opening before him.

Then he remembered, and as though a light was turned on inside by the Spirit, the words of our conversation came rushing back to him. "This is not the new me! I died with Christ—Christ is my new life, and here I am trying to answer this as if He wasn't there! Lord Jesus, this is *Your* problem. I don't want this—I recognize this to have already been dealt with at the cross—*You* are my life—live Your victory through me now."

How fast is prayer? The doors remained open waiting for another train to unload its passengers, but it was less than three minutes as José recognized the truth and rejected the lie. He recognized that Christ was his life and that the old him was dead. The truth sets us free (*see* John 8:32).

In that moment, José rose a new man, the new man he really was in Christ. The Spirit of the Lord came upon him and he began to praise God in tongues.

His words came back to me as we stood in his old habitat: "I just floated across the station, up the stairs, into the bank, and for two weeks I lived in that glory."

José was not seriously tempted on that point again. He had anchored his faith in the covenant and the area of testing moved elsewhere.

He turned to me and smiled. "Seen enough?" I nodded. I had seen a place where a man used to live, but he had died and stood beside me, united to Christ his life. He went on ahead of me, pushing past the cans and jumping the stairs—alive with an everlasting joy.

As he went on ahead of me, I remembered the very first term of covenant, and praisedGod for its reality. It seemed his feet beat out the tattoo on the bare boards: "I will put My law within them and on their hearts will I write it" (*see* Jeremiah 31:33).

As we stepped into the yellow sunlight that filtered through the smog, I gulped in the air, which was comparatively clear to what we had been breathing. I heard Ezekiel saying:

> Then I will sprinkle clean water on you, and you will be clean; I will cleanse you from all your filthiness and from all your idols. Moreover, I will give you a new heart and put a new spirit within you; and I will remove the heart of stone from your flesh and give you a heart of flesh. And I will put My Spirit within you and cause you to walk in My statutes. . . .
>
> Ezekiel 36:25–27

13
Living the Truth

This all sounds so wonderful. The trouble is that when we are in the thick of life we are inevitably faced with a choice around which everything hangs—the choice between our feelings and the truth.

There are high days when we look at the covenant terms and all seems very reasonable and workable. Then facing the office, the campus, and the screaming children we feel the whole thing is unworkable and the old-life pattern emerges.

If we are going to be *Diatheke* people, the expressions of the God we are in union with, we have got to see the difference between truth and our feelings about the truth. To act on truth just because I feel like it is really acting out of my feelings about the truth and not the truth itself.

It is the truth that sets us free—to know what God has done for me, and to choose to live in it is unlimited freedom (*see* John 8:32). But I must choose to live in that truth before I can enjoy the freedom.

The Lord Jesus stated that He is the Truth. He is the final uncovering of all fact, the Light in whom we see things as they really are. Only in Him do all facts square with reality. He is not some of the truth, He is *the* Truth.

Outside of Him I cannot know God as He really is. Only in the Lord Jesus Christ can I discover the true nature and purpose of the universe. There is no satisfactory answer to my own being until I discover myself in Jesus Christ.

Apart from Jesus Christ the world is in the darkness of the lie, imprisoned in the darkness. Man's ability to understand outside of Jesus Christ is very much like standing in a hall of mirrors. All the images are distorted, bearing little resemblance to a human being. Not that everything is wrong! You could still say that there is a mouth, ears, nose, eyes discernible.

So man's comprehension of the way things are is distorted by the great lie. He may have a few facts right but all is distorted and twisted. The great lie that started it all off at the beginning is, "I am at the center of the universe." While men believe that, their whole view of the universe is off—in darkness. All of my feelings will feed me information based on that.

In coming to Jesus Christ a man is faced with truth, light in the darkness. It can be a very painful experience to discover that God is not who I thought He was. I am not who I have been thinking I am. My existence is not for the reasons I had been building on. To confront Jesus Christ demands a total change of mind.

The word repentance means just that—literally, "an afterthought," or better, a change of mind. Confronted so, we resist truth, preferring to stay in the lie, enjoying the idea that we are at the center of the universe. "Men love darkness rather than light" (*see* John 3:19). To be saved is to receive the love of the truth, to agree that I have been all wrong, that

God is right and is fully revealed in Jesus Christ. It is to submit to the truth and turn from the sin of living according to the great lie.

So coming to the experience of the covenant is variously called, "obeying the truth" (1 Peter 1:22), "acknowledging of the truth" (2 Timothy 2:25), and "salvation through . . . belief of the truth" (2 Thessalonians 2:13).

It is not because I am offered a chance to be happy, although that is certainly a side benefit. It is rather a confrontation with truth that demands that I repent and confess that Jesus Christ is Lord.

Now begins the new life of living in the truth, living in union with God through Jesus Christ, which I have discovered is the true reason for my existence. It is a glorious new life, but one that clashes head-on with my habits formed in the old way, in the darkness. My feelings send me messages concerning life, concerning me, and I have to make the choice between truth as it is in Jesus, or my feelings.

Up until entering the covenant we live pretty much on our feelings. Our life is described as after the flesh, or a life lived out of feelings. Now I am confronted with a new set of facts, ultimate truth that makes my feelings into liars.

This battle is thrown into worse confusion because I have probably been given the impression that I am going to live this new life feeling great. Many rose to make a decision for Christ on the bait of a life of happiness and heaven. When they have feelings that are otherwise, they are thrown into confusion.

The covenant does not promise merely a set of happy feelings. It demands an adjustment of my whole life-style to the truth, in the power of the Holy Spirit who is within. That will many times be the reverse of what my feelings say. We crucify the flesh.

The way of the world is to act out of your feelings. The way of truth says act on the basis of truth and your feelings will follow. So 1 Peter 1:22 states that we purify our souls by *obeying* the truth. It is not merely agreeing that it is right but not feeling like it today. It is the obedience to God depending exclusively on the power of the Holy Spirit. So, ". . . work out your own salvation . . ." (Philippians 2:12 KJV). Obey the truth, put it into action, change your life-style to conform to the truth. How? ". . . with fear and trembling" (verse 12). That is, with no trust in yourself. You may have tried in your own strength and failed. Do not trust yourself. Your trust is: "For it is God which worketh in you both to will and to do of his good pleasure" (verse 13). God is at work willing His truth and He Himself is the power to do His truth. It is but for us to work it out.

Paul's letters to the churches never once appealed to how they felt. Always appealing to truth as it is in Jesus, he called them to act and obey. Not to walk in what they knew was truth was to walk in the lie, the darkness. We are ever choosing to be who we are.

Danny is a member of our church. He had been addicted to nicotine for ten years, smoking incessantly. When he came to Christ it was one of the first things the Lord checked him about—that his body, now the temple of the Spirit, should not be defiled. The night he was baptized in water, publicly declaring that he had entered the covenant, was indeed dead, and now buried to walk in new life, he felt that he should give up cigarettes—which he did for three days. He went back to smoking and stopping for about a year, around and around in circles, until he decided to leave the matter with God. His Baptism in the Spirit followed, but still he smoked. The Lord spoke to him in so many ways. That smoking had to be dealt with. It belonged to the world of lies where man needs outside stimulus for relaxation, whereas now in the truth the Spirit within us was all that was needed. Danny by this time didn't want to know. He refused to even pray about it.

He enjoyed smoking and didn't really want to stop. "Surely," he reasoned, "if God delivers me then I will not want to. It will be like having amnesia—I shall just wake up one morning and forget I ever liked cigarettes. If I stopped now it would be just me; I would be a hypocrite to act against my feelings." Feeling very justified and pious he continued to smoke.

His wife began to complain that he made the house smell like a trash can; his doctor told him he was a danger to his children's health. The pressure made him angry. Then some other members of the body mentioned his habit to him, which made him very angry. "Is smoking any worse than their sins?" he rationalized with himself. He avoided his own problem by looking at theirs. He began to avoid services that tended to be long, because he needed a smoke before they were through. His anger at everyone didn't encourage his attendance.

When anger subsided he came again to the Lord with his problem, weary of thinking, rationalizing, and warring because of it. It was then that the Lord showed him that what he had always thought of as deliverance didn't exist. He had been looking for a cop-out—looking for feelings to be on his side. He had to choose with an act of will to live truth and let his flesh be crucified, depending on God's power to carry through.

It was like a new revelation to him. In fact, it became easier than he had ever thought possible. Every time the desire to smoke came up he realized his union with God through Jesus Christ and chose to be controlled by truth, that God's will be done. There was a mortifying of his feelings regarding nicotine. He saw the essence of sin—putting his feelings before God's revealed truth. He received total victory over nicotine but through that moved into a new way of life, obedience to truth regardless of what his feelings said.

Many of us are not facing habits. Our battleground is the emergencies of love; wisdom to decide; our battle with adverse circumstaCES. In all those cases we face the lie and the truth. What do I feel about this?—which is usually the lie. And, who am I in covenant with God?—which is always the truth.

Viewing a circumstance that is accenting my weakness, I in myself tremble. There is an added temptation at this point, for I hear the suggestion that a good Christian would not tremble at this. I might run off to the Law to be strong in myself if I listened. Instead I recognize that I will always be weak in myself, but the truth is united with strength Himself, and I am strong with His strength.

Faced with a need to love, we feel our inadequacy—in fact feel the stirrings of "unlove." We do not go into a despair but confess the truth—that God in union with me is love within and through me.

The matter of God's will is of great concern to many. They are ever searching and putting out fleeces, afraid that we shall miss the will of God. How can we if we are united with God Himself, who is one with His purpose? We confess that in Christ we are one with eternal wisdom and refuse the fears of missing His will. We check with the principles of the Scripture and move out through the doors that are providentially open, believing that we have the mind of Christ.

This attitude of acknowledging the truth and refusing the lie that our feelings are ever about to believe becomes our life-style. Many of us have trained ourselves for years to tune in to the morning broadcast of our feelings. We have a torrent of lies to wake up to. "It's going to be a bad day. Another day of defeat. I am sure everything is going wrong," etc., etc. The covenant man has learned to replace the lie with the truth.

While counseling with a brother who didn't know his place in the covenant, he interspersed his description of the problem by reiterating, "It's no use, I can't do it. I've always had this problem and I guess I always will." He did not realize the facts of the covenant, that when he had believed into the Lord Jesus Christ he had died with His death. That old person who couldn't do it, who certainly had that problem, had died and had been buried in baptism. His life was now Christ in him, but he believed what he felt, and believed the testimony of his past more than the testimony of God. He never rose above this testimony.

The covenant man thinks of himself as he really is in Christ. He learns to look at situations from that position. He learns that this is the way things *really* are. He gradually drops the old, independent way of thinking and it becomes easy to think of himself in covenant relationship.

He rises in the morning praising God, that God is his Father, and this day is in His hands. He praises God that he is the righteousness of God in him, and that today all things work together for good. He worships his Father who is love, wisdom, almighty power—and ever with him, who will never leave him or forsake him. He looks at life and shouts through all his soul, "I can do all things through Christ who strengthens me" (*see* Philippians 4:13). He looks at the pressures and problems of life and worships his Father, who cares for the birds and will surely care for him today. He walks out into the world aware that today, because Christ is in him, he is the light of the world, the salt of the earth (*see* Matthew 5:13, 14), and just by being alive in covenant relationship will turn his neighbors' eyes toward heaven.

This man can face the pressures from people because he knows now what life is all about. Every man and circumstance that causes an old-life reaction, a reaction of fear or helplessness, can now be received with joy from the hands of the Holy Spirit, who is bringing about a greater conformity to the death of Jesus so that the life of Jesus may flow more easily and radiantly.

Whenever this man looks at his past, however bad, he glories in the fact that God should be such love that He loved him, the blood be so sufficient that he has been cleansed, the covenant so glorious that even he is brought into a new fellowship with the Father. His past cannot condemn him but only serve as a springboard for yet more exulting in God.

Does this man ever fall? Yes, but he knows why, which is half the battle. He knows that if he operates out of himself instead of out of God, he will immediately crash. But he knows that the Scripture has made provision: "If we confess our sins, He is faithful and righteous to forgive us our sins and to cleanse us from all unrighteousness" (1 John 1:9). This he does, and gets up daring to believe that he is forgiven and the matter is dealt with. He refuses the devil's accusations and condemnations, knowing that he is a liar and the blood of Jesus cleanses from all sin.

If this man in his fall hurts another, he will go and confess the matter to the one he has hurt and ask to be forgiven even as he has been forgiven by God.

Such a man walks in the peace of God that passes and baffles all human understanding. He rejoices in the joy of God that is unspeakable and unexplainable, having no connection to the circumstances around, and this man loves with the love of God which is shed abroad in his heart by the Holy Spirit.

Walk awhile with such a man and you get the impression he is from another planet, for he is in the world—but certainly not of it. He seems to be a stranger and a pilgrim here. You would be right, for he has exited the world by death and has returned in resurrection, Christ now being his life. The believer is a strange fellow. *He is not who he feels he is, he is who he is in Jesus Christ.* Happy covenant man, living in unbroken fellowship with the Three-in-One.

By what I have said in describing the covenant man it may be thought that I expect him to live at a screaming high all the time. Absolutely not. The joy, peace, and love of God is not something that is always giggling like a group of teen-age girls! It is deep and does not always express itself in a grinning face—but rather has a stabilizing effect on all of life, spreading a mature peace through all activity and thought, causing a joy to quietly radiate through everything said, done, and anticipated.

But again someone says, "But I don't feel like that all the time." Nor do I! But we have learned not to live out of our feelings, but out of God, who is our all.

A few weeks ago I was conducting a seminar in an upstate city. The circumstances I was facing at that time were crushing, and I had no reason to feel filled with joy. My feelings were at an all-time low. I *felt* that heaven had become hidden, and the covenant did not exist. But I knew that this was a lie and I chose not to believe it. If I had chosen to believe it, I would have been under the authority of that lie so long as I chose to accept it.

Instead I chose truth and made the truth my constant confession. It kept me stable throughout that week. Every waking moment I lived on the confession of truth and never once did the feelings take authority. At the end of the week I suddenly experienced a *feeling of the facts.*

One of the only hobbies I have is fishing and I sometimes describe it as the lie game—not lying about the size of my fish. The whole operation is based on the fish believing my lie. I put a dead worm in the water and my success depends entirely on whether the fish will believe that it is a real, live worm. If I can make them believe that what is dead is really alive, then I will have them hooked. Apart from this I have no other power over the fish. The devil is a great fisher. He drops feelings and ideas from your past into the pool of your mind and waits for you to accept it as a real, living, now fact.

If you see it for what it is, dead with Christ, you can discard it as the lie it is—but if you accept the lie then you are hooked under the authority of that lie so long as you accept it. The devil only has as much power as you choose to give him.

We have found that people who have a life-style of sin and failure must start thinking what is true. "Whatsoever things are true . . . think on these things" (Philippians 4:8). Replace the expectancy of defeat with the expectancy that God will keep His terms laid down in the sacred *Berith*.

A sister in the Lord called me the other day to ask advice concerning a family problem. It boiled down to a few simple facts: a misunderstanding between the lady and a relative, a few sharp exchanges, and a no-talking sign outside their lives. Bitterness had begun to smolder and she wanted advice.

"That's simple," I replied. "You must confess your sin of unlove to the Lord and receive forgiveness. You must then go to the person you have wronged and ask her forgiveness."

"Hey, wait a minute, wait a minute!" she interrupted. "*She* did the wrong, not me, and anyway I don't feel like forgiving her, and if I did it without feeling it, it would be insincere —I would be a hypocrite, wouldn't I?"

"Let's get some things straight," I countered. "Number one—whatever her sin is against you is her problem! *You* have unlove, and it is obvious you are harboring real bitterness—that is what you must ask her forgiveness for. You must return love, God's love, for whatever she did to you."

"But I can't—I don't feel any love for her at all," she replied rather helplessly.

"Look! You are a blood-covenant woman and the fact is

that Christ is in you—and He is love—I am not telling you to try to love her, I am telling you to love her with *God's love*. And as to your feelings, God's love is not a warm, mushy feeling, but action, costly action. The feelings follow the action."

There was silence, then, "Okay, what do I do?"

"Put this phone down and receive forgiveness from the Lord. Then thank the Father that Christ *does* live in you and He is love, and in His name you are going to love the woman and ask forgiveness."

The line went dead. Twenty minutes later she was back on the telephone elated. She had done everything I had suggested and fellowship had been restored between the two. "And you know," she said enthusiastically, "as soon as I did it, I *felt* something—I felt warm and—and *good*. I see what you mean now."

14
Expressers of Christ

We are now in a position to grasp the grand purposes of God. He has chosen that we shall be His expressions on earth, a body of people in *Berith* who are not only in union but also the expressers of His purpose.

The fact that we have come to believe certain things about God and His purposes in Jesus Christ; the fact that we have a relationship to Him through Christ is only the beginning, the foundation. The aim and goal of covenant is such a company on earth who are now thinkers of His thoughts, speakers of His Word, and doers of His acts. God has His new man on earth, the church, the executor of His will.

The Scripture uses the illustration of the head and the body to describe the relationship between Christ and the church. My head and body are one. But the head is the source of life, the body the expression of that life. So Christ is the life and we the expressers of Him on earth.

If I wish to do something for you, it is only a wish until I express it through my body. So God has chosen that He will execute His will through the minds, lips, and bodies of His finite creatures who have been raised to *Berith* relationship. Our union with Him is the foundation of our expressing Him.

Another illustration Jesus used was the vine and branches (*see* John 15). This is the picture of the relationship between Christ and the believer. This underlines the enormity of what the grand purpose of God is. What is the vine, if it doesn't include the branches? The branches are not something separate from the vine, *they are the expressing part of the vine.* When I speak of a vine I always assume it has branches! So God has chosen that joined to Christ we shall be the expressers of Him on the earth.

God has chosen to accomplish His work on earth through His *Berith* partner, the new man in Christ. Through our lips speaking His will, His glory shall be known in the earth.

This is a far cry from a church that is ever whimpering to a distant God about how bad things are, and asking Him to please do something. This is the church in union, the church in communion, which knows His will and speaks—"Thy will be done on earth as it is in heaven" (*see* Matthew 6:10).

A church may go into all the world proclaiming the Good News of the New Covenant, but as it does so it is the expresser of that finished work. If it meets devils it casts them out; if it is confronted with the sick it lays hands on them and heals them; if it is hindered by anything in the animal or vegetable world it speaks it out of the way—for it is the expresser of God's purpose, not only enjoying it and speaking of it.

So we face the people of the world, not only telling them that they are loved of God, but also to be that love to them. We do not speak of a Jesus who rose as merely a character of far-off history. We are His extension on earth. In meeting the church they meet His body, and in our words and acts have a vital meeting with Him.

This idea runs through all of Paul's letters. He wrote:

> Therefore in Christ Jesus I have found reason for boasting
> in things pertaining to God. For I will not presume to speak
> of anything except what *Christ has accomplished through
> me,* resulting in the obedience of the Gentiles by word and
> deed, in the power of signs and wonders, in the power of the
> Spirit; so that from Jerusalem and round about as far as
> Illyricum I have fully preached the gospel of Christ.
>
> Romans 15:17–19

It was not Paul doing a job of work for God out of his own
brain and intellect, but rather Christ doing the work through
Paul. The initiative and the enablement was Christ vitally
united to him.

He shows up most clearly in such expressions as in this
version of 1 Thessalonians 1:6: "You also became imitators of
us and of the Lord." They not only proclaimed the Word,
they were its living demonstration, for they were one with it.
Or again, in 1 Corinthians 11: "Be imitators of me, just as I
am also of Christ" (*see* verse 1), and 1 Corinthians 4: "For
if you were to have countless tutors in Christ, yet you would
not have many fathers; for in Christ Jesus I became your
father through the gospel. I exhort you therefore, be imitators of me" (*see* verses 15, 16).

Paul not only held his life up as a living example of Christ's
teaching, but also sent Timothy to "remind you of my ways"
(*see* verse 17). He sent him specifically to *be* among them

what the teaching *said*. This is repeated, widening the horizon of models in Philippians 3:17: "Brethren, join in following my example, and observe those who walk according to the pattern you have in us."

Paul summed up his method of teaching in 2 Thessalonians 3:7–9:

> For you yourselves know how you ought to follow our example; because we did not act in an undisciplined manner among you, nor did we eat anyone's bread without paying for it, but with labor and hardship we kept working night and day so that we might not be a burden to any of you; not because we do not have the right to this, but in order to offer ourselves as a model for you, that you might follow our example.

He laid it down as a principle that they should follow his example, then reminded them of that example and finished by stating that he was the message in flesh form. God is coming to the people in the Word, but also in His covenant man. This principle was outlined in Philippians 4:9: "The things you have learned and received and heard and seen in me, practice these things. . . ." Paul reminded them that they heard *and also saw in him* the things that they had learned.

We are not merely microphones. We are those who speak out of our unity. This is expected of all Christians, not just the elite of the body, for Paul wrote to the young Thessalonians in his first letter (1:7) that they had become an example to all the countryside around.

This is no theory. We are containers and expressers of love

Himself. We are that love in Christ. That love died for us. It is love with no limit, love to the nth—love with no reason, for God is His own reason for loving. That love is now in us, and is displayed in our actions.

Paul had entered the body of Christ propelled by such a *modeling* of this love. He not only heard of love that had died for him, but he *touched* that love in Stephen. Stephen was reviled and dragged through the streets of the city at the order of Saul, and then as the stones were hurled at him he prayed, "Lord, lay not this sin to their charge" (Acts 7:60 KJV). That was the love of God in Stephen form; a man united with God to, in a sense, be God in that moment.

I remember the day I saw this so clearly. Walking down a dark, narrow street in London I was suddenly blinded by the sun. The glare made me shield my eyes—very normal, except I was in a dark street. Then I saw a little fellow in an open alley with a mirror in his hand. By tilting the mirror so as to have a right relationship to the sun, he actually brought the sun into that street. I was blinded momentarily, not by the mirror but by the sun that was in that mirror, and through the mirror so perfectly reflected that *for the moment I confronted the sun, not the mirror.*

In ourselves we are nothings, creatures of the dust, never able or meant to be anything *in ourselves,* but given a right relationship to the Three-in-One through the covenant, we become so one with Him that people confront Him in us, and bypass us and actually have a meeting with Him. Jesus said, "I am the light of the world. . ." (John 8:12). He also said in Matthew 5:14, "You are the light of the world. . . ." The sun is the light of our natural planet, and given the right relationship a mirror can so contain and express the sun that it too is the light of the planet with the light of the sun. So we in covenant union are lights that shine in the darkness. We shine with Christ's own light:

> Do all things without grumbling or disputing; that you may prove yourselves to be blameless and innocent, children of God above reproach in the midst of a crooked and perverse generation, among whom you appear as lights in the world.
>
> Philippians 2:14, 15

We not only *have* the message, we *are it.*

When explaining his actions in 2 Corinthians 5:14, Paul said that the love of Christ controlled him. Not a love like Christ's or a great concern for people, but the love *of Christ Himself* controlled him. The Greek word for control is a medical term used to describe a person under the control of a fever. Paul was "fevered" with Christ's love so greatly that his thinking, planning, words, and actions were the love of Christ before men.

We often have a false humility which is really pride. We think that to say such things about oneself would be arrogant. Our trouble is that we have such a low view of what God has accomplished that we would rather call God a liar and see ourselves as mere humans trying to do something for God. God calls us His people, expressers of His glory because of what Christ has done. Humility is seeing things as they *really are* and taking my place in that scheme of things. The way things really are in Christ is that *Christ in me is now confronting the world.* That is the humble statement of every body of believers.

It revolutionizes our attitudes to the world and the people we meet every day. God wishes to speak with them, to show Himself for who He really is, so He walks into their office in me; onto their campus in me; and begins to show Himself in me. He walks me into places where impatience would be natural so that He can display His patience; He calls me to express that love in dying for them in a thousand little ways. We no longer chaff at the smallness of our lives. Can anything be small if God has walked me into it to specifically live Himself in me at that point?

In the same way we are the eyes of God, the ears of God, and the mouth of God. Because He is our new eyesight we see that things are not what they seem to be. We become seers. Every time we meet an emergency or confront a need, we see not the need but an opportunity for God, the eternal supply, to fill it. We are united to that supply, and we are the speaking end of it on earth and so we speak out of Him, His supply, and watch as the need is swallowed up.

Did Jesus ever see need alone? Did He not rather see the supply filling the need? Did Jesus really see the great need of thousands of people without food, or did He see there but an opportunity for His Father's ever-present fullness to be manifested? Did He see sickness alone, or did he see it rather as the opportunity for His Father's life-health to be displayed? The church has become shortsighted and speaks in terms of need and emptiness. All supply is ours in our union. It is but for us to speak it into existence with our words of faith.

Faith is our response to God's supply. For years I thought that I had to believe and so make God do something. The covenant teaches me God has done all, He is now my supply, and I am saying *Thank you.* Faith is when, looking at the need, I see the supply and say *Thank you.* The shortsighted man who can only see the need thinks I am crazy.

So we are not forever sending petitions to God that He would do something. Rather we are speakers of what He has done. Too many hours are wasted in reading our celestial shopping lists to God. We should have been speaking the supply into the needs that He had walked us into.

Two Corinthians 1:20 is of vital importance here: "For as many as may be the promises of God, in Him they are yes; wherefore also by Him is our Amen to the glory of God through us." Paul explains that the vast resources of God's promises are all a plain yes because of our relationship in Christ. What must we do then if God is saying, "Yes, I mean it," after every promise? We must supply the *Amen*—which means "So be it." Every time God says a yes in His Word, we say on earth, "It shall be done." The result? "To the glory of God." God's glory is known on the earth and note that it has to be through us, for that is how He has chosen to work.

Israel trembled before Goliath. They saw a problem and wrote home for prayer support. Cringing in the trenches they expected God's power to mysteriously hit them and give them a high so that they would not notice the impossibilities in front of them. This never came, so they trembled before the words of Goliath waiting for God to show up and do something.

David showed up and did something. God showed up in David! David saw with God's eyes, and spoke with God's words. The Israelite soldiers saw the problem. David saw it too; he also saw the covenant that stated that this land was given by God to them, and therefore could never be taken, and he also saw that in covenant to touch them was to touch God.

He, in union with God, walked out as if that were true, and spoke not out of his own resources but out of God their strength. He spoke to Goliath as if the whole thing was as good as done. It was only minutes before it was.

Any boy from the army could have done that, for they were all in covenant. Only one, who was not old enough for the draft, realized that for him to be in a situation was for God to be in it and it was up to him to take the principles of God's covenant promises and apply them to the local situation with an *Amen*.

You are where you are God's love, light, and life reaching to those around you, not merely in words, but in you expressing Christ. You are there to speak the promises of God into being, for He said, "I will be your God, and you will be My people" (*see* Jeremiah 31:33).